D0064831

"Ron Susek's insights flow from the crucible of the testing battles accompanying his many years of effective ministry. His biblically sound doctrinal and theological understandings are evident in each devotional. These short studies induce deep spiritual thinking. Those intent on developing a prayer life that pleases God and brings his sovereign answers will rejoice to use this weekly guide. I look forward to using it in the continuing enhancement of my own practice of prayer."

Dr. Mark I. Bubeck, president emeritus
International Center for Biblical Counseling
Sun City, Arizona

"Do you want to fill your year with blessings? Get this meditation workbook on the subject of prayer. God has been teaching Ron Susek many truths, which he shares here. His suggestions will provoke your careful thought and grateful meditation, challenge you to a more active and comprehensive life of prayer, and deepen your walk with the Lord. There is one challenge to your spiritual life for each week of the year. Don't just rush through it. Pray, meditate, and grow through it."

Dr. Wesley Duewel, president emeritus
OMS International
Greenwood, Indiana

God Will Answer

52 Meditations
to Enrich Your Prayer Life

Ron Susek

Baker Books

A Division of Baker Book House Co
Grand Rapids, Michigan 49516

Published by Baker Books
a division of Baker Book House Company
P.O. Box 6287, Grand Rapids, MI 49516-6287

Printed in the United States of America

Library of Congress Cataloging-in-Publication Data

Susek, Ron.
    God will answer : 52 meditations to enrich your prayer life / Ron Susek.
      p.   cm.
    ISBN 0-8010-1228-7 (cloth)
    1. Prayer—Christianity—Meditations. 2. Christian life—Baptist authors. I. Title.
  BV220 .S87 2001
  242'.2—dc21
                                              2001025943

For current information about all releases from Baker Book House, visit our web site:
http://www.bakerbooks.com

To all who are committed
as people of prayer,
and especially to you who are
part of the prayer team that
regularly holds this ministry
before God. You have stood
with me through some
amazing battles and victories,
and I thank you.

"Which of you fathers, if your son asks for a fish,
will give him a snake instead? Or if he asks
for an egg, will give him a scorpion?
If you then, though you are evil,
know how to give good gifts to your children,
how much more will your Father in heaven
give the Holy Spirit to those who ask him?"

Jesus Christ
Luke 11:11–13

Contents

The Thrill
of Communing with God

God promised to answer prayer, pledging to do so on the basis of his own character, even sealing his commitment in the blood of his Son. Can he fail? Will he neglect your need? Would he ever treat you as unimportant?

No! Impossible! God has promised to answer prayer, and so he will.

But prayer is far more than merely getting answers from God. Prayer develops the soul, establishes God's will, and impacts people and events on earth. Since prayer is the gateway to heaven, it opens an eternal horizon that may take eternity to explore fully.

In September of 1979, I resolved to learn how to pray for one hour each day. It was then that I made two startling discoveries. First, there was a deep restlessness in my spirit. I squirmed like a confined brat. I met myself head-on, and the sight wasn't pretty. It took months before that sense of confinement was transformed into the thrill of conquest. That conquest developed into a sense of communion.

Second, my expectations were shattered when, instead of finding myself on majestic mountains with God, I landed smack dab in the middle of a spiritual desert. I would learn that prayer is a war—a war in which the big battles are fought and won by engagement, or lost by default.

Working in Gettysburg, Pennsylvania, where the decisive battle of the Civil War was fought, has taught me this major principle of war: Only fight from high ground. General Robert E. Lee attacked the Union army at Gettysburg while they occupied the high ground.

Lee lost.

Christ has given us the high ground. We're seated with him in the heavenly realms, free to address God at any moment. It doesn't get any higher than that. From this position of strength, we reign over our enemies, gaining great victories through prayer.

I, for one, wanted to prove God's willingness to answer prayer—even overcome impossible situations. Perseverance prevailed! In time, prayer became intriguing beyond compare. Nothing could match the exhilaration of affecting events through my blood-bought right to pray. Over the following years I experienced times when prayer seemed powerless, and other times when it moved the mountain of impossibility. Soon it became evident that there's nothing God cannot (or will not) change through prayer—on *his* schedule and in *his* way.

I started writing the thoughts found in this book on scraps of paper and in the margins of my Bible, primarily for myself. Then, in the spring of 1997, I was silenced by a vocal problem that threatened to end my speaking ministry. Since I was forbidden to speak, my wife pinned a message on my clothes that read, COMPLETE VOCAL REST. I wrote notes to store clerks expressing what I wanted. Assuming that muteness also meant deafness (and dumbness), they spoke loudly, forming their words carefully, as one would to a two-year-old: "You want soap? All right, dear, I'll get it for you. You want help to carry the bag?"

I'm not sure if God healed me to preach again or to deliver me from such kindness, but this period gave me the opportunity to start writing about prayer. For four months my fingers replaced my voice, and my computer replaced the pulpit. The results are now in your hands.

Here's how to use this book: Resist the temptation to read ahead and read just one meditation each week. Then reread the text each weekday, commune with God in prayer, and focus on daily questions. This will enable you to digest the concept and make it your own. Finally, make the commitment and stay with it.

I hope your prayer life will be enriched through this weekly time together. If you wish, one year from today, drop me a note telling of the things you've learned, and add the answers God granted to you throughout the year.

Will God answer you? Indeed, he will!

The First Prayer

God, have mercy on me, a sinner.

Luke 18:13

God gave ten commandments clearly stating what not to do. There are no corresponding ten commandments of what to do.

Why so? There are two important reasons: First, God's commands are given not to rob human freedom, but to protect it. God made you to be a free agent—not free in the sense of doing your own thing, but free to enter the wide expanse of possibilities found in serving his will. Jesus said that knowing the truth would set you free. You will be unhindered!

Second, God made you to be a cocreator with him. Unlike ants that march without choice to do chores that satisfy nothing but programmed instincts, you're given the power to think, reason, remember, forget, feel, plan, and dream! While not an eye has seen nor ear heard of the things that lie in your eternal future, you'll never grasp in this lifetime the creative expanse God has placed before you.

So then, how do the Ten Commandments fit into this picture? They're given not to limit you but to protect you from limiting yourself. Sin imprisons and stifles creativity. Conversely, obedience empowers and releases creativity. E. Stanley Jones, a famed missionary to India, expressed it in words like these: When you disobey, the laws of the universe resist you. When you obey, they move with you.

Herein is the problem: All have sinned (Rom. 3:23). Jesus said, "Everyone who sins is a slave to sin" (John 8:34). Ecclesiastes 8:8 expresses the enslaving power of sin this way: "As no one is discharged in time of war, so wickedness will not release those who practice it." In short, not only were you born imprisoned by sin, but even after redemption in Christ you'll do things that will slam prison doors on your freedom and creativity.

The starting point or first prayer, then, is the cry for mercy. This cry invokes a sympathetic response from God to release you from the loss of freedom and reduced creativity resulting from sin. It's the recognition that you can't undo the past that's undoing you, but you recognize God can and will intervene. He has the power not only to forgive, but to change hearts and circumstances. He has the power (and desire) to set you free to serve him with full creativity.

Generally, mercy is readily extended to one who has unfairly fallen victim to an enemy. But you may be the victim of your own willful sin. In this case, appealing to God for mercy is asking for something completely undeserved. You wonder if God will consider your plea. You hope to touch a nerve of sympathetic kindness.

Indeed, God is rich in mercy. He has a heart that can be touched. His mercy is rooted in a covenant with you. To state it as strongly as possible: God has sealed his covenant of love, including his abundant mercy, in the blood of his Son. Thus, "Mercy triumphs over judgment!" (James 2:13). God is faithful to his covenant even when mankind is unfaithful.

The first prayer to God, then, even for the most advanced saint, is, "Be merciful to me, a sinner." When God's mercy meets with your confession and repentance, prison doors open. Creativity is once again released to run and play in the open spaces of divine freedom.

■ COMMUNE WITH GOD ■

Father, I ask you first of all for your mercy as I confront and confess my sins. Break sin's power to imprison me. Help me love your laws—laws given to protect my freedom and release my creativity.

▪ MAKE THE TEXT YOUR OWN ▪

Day One: What key thought do you wish to remember from this meditation?

Day Two: Jesus said that knowing truth would set you free. In what ways do you desire the Lord to set you free?

Day Three: What do you see in yourself as the biggest enemy (or obstacle) to finding God's gifts of freedom and creativity?

Day Four: The Lord delights in our honesty. Ask him how to overcome the obstacles that prohibit you from living a more abundant life.

Day Five: When God's mercy meets with your confession and repentance, creativity is once again released to run and play in the open spaces of divine freedom. In what ways do you feel you have been set free to greater creativity?

Nothing Between: Prepare for Prayer

I said, "I will confess my transgressions to the
LORD"—and you forgave the guilt of my sin.
Therefore let everyone who is godly pray to
you.

Psalm 32:5–6

No Old Testament high priest ever rushed unprepared into the Holy of Holies; after all, his life depended upon proper preparation. Once a year he was privileged to step behind the curtain and into God's presence to make atonement for the people's sins committed during the previous year. He would prepare by offering sacrifices for his own sins and by washing his clothes and body. Only then did he step behind the curtain. If he failed in any part of his preparation, he would fall to his death in the holy presence of God.

But a wondrous event changed all that when Jesus Christ died. A bolt of lightning sliced the curtain of the temple in half, and the most crude, vulgar sinner could look into the Holy of Holies without consequence. Why? Because the most holy place had been moved into the heavenly realms—the place you enter when you pray. You're invited to enter God's presence ceaselessly (1 Thess. 5:17), boldly, and confidently (Heb. 10:19–22). But never are you invited to come dirty, that is, unless you're planning to be cleansed of the dirt!

Where did you get the idea that you can run into God's throne room like a child dragging muddy shoes through the house? Do you assume that God's grace allows you to approach him smeared with the remains of a peanut butter and jelly sandwich, as though he should find this cute? Have you no sense of awe, no sense of stepping before purity when you pray?

Preparing to pray is more than good manners. It's more important than a child learning to leave muddy shoes at the door. It's the practice of having nothing between your soul and the Savior. You're coming before the Creator, the Ancient of Days, who cannot look lightly upon sin.

So, how do you prepare to enter a place of absolute moral and spiritual purity? First, learn to pray as did David: "Search me, O God, and know my heart; test me and know my anxious thoughts. See if there is any offensive way in me, and lead me in the way everlasting" (Ps. 139:23–24). This is not morbid introspection. It's asking God to do the searching and revealing. Only then can you fulfill the next step: confession.

What is confession? It's agreeing with God against yourself. It's refusing to offer excuses and explanations to God, such as, "The reason I am this way is because of what others have done to me." Confession simply declares, "I'm guilty of the sin you've revealed."

God's work begins with forgiving and cleansing you. Forgiveness is instant. In the sense of changing you, however, the cleansing is generally progressive. All the same, you have the immediate right to enter God's presence, made clean by the blood of Jesus Christ.

Prepare, then, to enter God's presence. Honor him by freshly cleansing your hands and feet. Clear your heart of clutter and sin like a disciplined child not wanting to drag dirt through the house.

David wrote in Psalm 11:4–5: "The LORD is in his holy temple; the LORD is on his heavenly throne. He observes the sons of men; his eyes examine them. The LORD examines the righteous, but the wicked and those who love violence his soul hates." Please the Almighty, then. Come to him properly prepared, with nothing between your heart and his.

■ COMMUNE WITH GOD ■

Father, there's no experience in life so invigorating, whole, complete, or fulfilling as to experience oneness with you. Help me to keep nothing between us. I have confessed, I am cleansed, and I thank you for this privilege. Draw near to me and remind me in all my humanness to draw near to you.

■ MAKE THE TEXT YOUR OWN ■

Day One: What key thought do you wish to remember from this meditation?

Day Two: Confession is an agreement with God against yourself. In what areas of your life have you chosen to side with God instead of yourself?

Day Three: In what ways can you relate to the phrase "running into God's throne room like a child dragging muddy shoes through the house?"

Day Four: "Search me, O God, and know my heart; test me and know my anxious thoughts. See if there is any offensive way in me, and lead me in the way everlasting" (Ps. 139:23–24). List five steps you can take to enter God's throne room in a worthy manner.

Day Five: In what area of your life do you find yourself blaming others for your attitudes or actions, rather than taking full responsibility?

The Work of Christ as You Pray

Christ Jesus . . . is at the right hand of God and
is also interceding for us.

Romans 8:34

Although I've met a few important people over the years (governors, presidents, prime ministers), only once did I do so without an intercessor. That was a mistake. I was young and brash at the time. As a student at Washington Bible College, I periodically attended the same church as President Lyndon Baines Johnson (you've got me dated now). One Sunday, as he stood by his limousine at the close of a service, I walked up to him, took his arm, and started to say, "Mr. President, I'm praying for you."

Notice, I only started to say this. The words weren't out of my mouth when secret service agents, still edgy from President Kennedy's assassination, stepped between the President and me. The President was put into his long, black limousine, sirens screamed, and the motorcade roared toward the White House. I stood there feeling like the world's biggest fool. Never again did I consider meeting an important person without being properly presented by an intermediary.

Approaching God is infinitely greater than meeting a mere mortal. There's no way to enter his presence without Jesus Christ, your High Priest, interceding and establishing your full right to be there, a right he paid for with his blood. Just as there is no other name under heaven given among men by which you are saved (Acts 4:12), so there is no person who has the rightful position to intercede for you other than Jesus Christ. Jesus:

Introduces you to his Father.

Intercepts Satan's accusations.

Intercedes for your needs.

There are two ways you can insult Christ. One is to think you can enter God's presence without him as your High Priest and intercessor, believing you can come before God on your own merit. All the world over, man-made religions and cults shape God into their own image, then approach him on their own terms. The French essayist Montaigne expressed this impudence: "O senseless man who cannot make a worm, and yet makes gods by the dozens."

The other insult is to approach God in some name other than Christ's. Millions of people ask biblical characters or deceased saints to pray for them, something the Bible never endorses. Others think they can use the name of Jesus to command God to fulfill their latest whim. This is also a practice outside of Scripture. These are not merely mistakes, they insult the High Priest, Jesus Christ, the one and only intercessor.

Ponder Hebrews 4:14–16: "Therefore, since we have a great high priest who has gone through the heavens, Jesus the Son of God, let us hold firmly to the faith we profess. For we do not have a high priest who is unable to sympathize with our weaknesses, but we have one who has been tempted in every way, just as we are—yet was without sin. Let us then approach the throne of grace with confidence, so that we may receive mercy and find grace to help us in our time of need."

■ COMMUNE WITH GOD ■

Father, thank you that, by grace, you've provided a worthy intercessor, through whom I have complete access to both your throne and heart. Jesus, thank you for making yourself human, leaving heaven to clear the way for me to come directly to God. Heavenly Father, Holy Son, know my love for you. Thank you for your presence.

■ Make the Text Your Own ■

Day One: What key thought do you wish to remember from this meditation?

Day Two: How does this week's meditation help you see the importance of closing your prayer, "In Jesus' name"?

Day Three: How might you pray in a way that honors and brings joy to Jesus Christ?

Day Four: "Christ Jesus . . . is at the right hand of God and is also interceding for us" (Rom. 8:34). How might you become more aware of Christ's role in your life as great High Priest?

Day Five: Jesus introduces you to his Father, intercepts Satan's accusations, and intercedes for your needs. How do Zechariah 3 and Revelation 12:10 further solidify your thoughts about Christ as your intercessor?

The Work of the Holy Spirit as You Pray

The Spirit himself intercedes for us.

Romans 8:26

Some years ago my wife, Diane, and I were about to land in Calgary, Alberta, amid a blinding snowstorm when a flight attendant came to my seat and said, "The captain has invited you to the cockpit for the landing." To this day I don't have a clue what inspired this, but I gladly followed him.

Soon I was strapped into a seat behind the pilot and copilot, staring with wide-eyed wonderment. Snow sprayed across the window, deepening the gray wall outside. Nothing was visible more than one inch beyond the windshield. I started asking questions.

"What's that instrument?" I queried. It was a longitudinal line that moved from left to right.

"There's a signal coming up from the middle of the runway," the pilot explained. "As long as that line is in the center of the circle, we're lined up dead center with the runway."

"And what's that instrument?" I asked, pointing to the one with airplane wings that rose above and fell beneath a horizontal line.

He explained, "Coming up from the runway, there's another signal that gives us a proper rate of descent. As long as we keep those wings on that horizontal line, we're descending at a proper rate for landing."

I thought, what an incredible illustration of the twofold work of the Holy Spirit. Paul wrote in Romans 8:26, "The Spirit helps us in our weakness. We do not know what we ought to pray for, but the Spirit himself intercedes for us with groans that words cannot express."

What, then, is the Holy Spirit doing? He begins by discovering the Father's will for every matter in life. Paul wrote in 1 Corinthians 2:10, "The Spirit searches all things, even the deep things of God." Knowing the mind of the Father, the Holy Spirit searches your heart. Then, even when you do not know what to pray for, the Holy Spirit aligns your prayers in the center of God's will and gives them a proper descent into God's heart. Romans 8:27 records, "The Spirit intercedes for the saints in accordance with God's will."

What does this mean to you? Do you often find yourself in a threatening situation, flying blindly through a snowstorm, trying to land on solid ground? You may feel that prayer is futile because you hardly know what to ask for. The storm may be so intense that all you can see is deep gray one inch in front of you. At times you can only utter a whisper, sometimes only a groan. But all the while the Holy Spirit is aligning your prayers, as feeble and confused as they may be, dead center with God's will. In short, you can't miss!

I felt nervous as we descended toward the airport at Calgary, looking at a windshield thick with mucky gray slush. Yet in time I saw runway lights streaking past us on each side, and I felt a slight tremor as the wheels touched down. It all happened by faith in the instruments, not by sight. So it is when you trust the Holy Spirit to do his work as you pray through the storms of your life.

▪ COMMUNE WITH GOD ▪

Thank you, Father, for granting help as I pray. Find me faithful in prayer, knowing that your Holy Spirit faithfully works for me, with me. Thank you that, even in my weakness, my prayers can find your will.

■ MAKE THE TEXT YOUR OWN ■

Day One: What key thought do you wish to remember from this meditation?

Day Two: What storm are you currently facing in which you do not know how to pray? What comfort do you find from this week's lesson?

Day Three: As the pilot must trust the instruments of the plane, so we must trust in God's Word and character when we are in the midst of confusion and turmoil. What are your feelings saying today about your present testing? What must you determine to do in order to land safely in your current turbulence?

Day Four: Jot down how the Holy Spirit assists you. In what ways do you believe life would be different without God's Spirit making intercession for you?

Day Five: "The Spirit himself intercedes for us" (Rom. 8:26). What assurance do you find in knowing that the Trinity is discussing how to demonstrate his love and encourage you today?

WEEK 5 TO ENRICHMENT

Know Him

I know whom I have believed.

2 Timothy 1:12

Prayer isn't awakening a slumbering God to the realities of your passing crisis. It's opening your eyes to see God's plan, established in eternity past. God saw your problem back when his Son decided to go to the cross, and eventually Christ died to make the answer possible.

Why, then, do you get the feeling that God is putting your need on hold? Because you expect him to fulfill your desired solution at the expense of his desired purpose? His purpose is that you should come to know him more deeply in the midst of the problem. You're asking him for a resolution; he's asking you for a relationship.

What's more, God seeks to draw you into his greater plan for your life. Strangely, however, when life works out to your liking, you may be struck with a sudden case of spiritual narcolepsy, dead asleep to God's plan.

Prayer is the primary way that you can rise above the mundane maze of life and engage in God's eternal plan and purpose: "To bring all things in heaven and on earth together under one head, even Christ" (Eph. 1:10).

Just as the cross was not a surprise to Jesus—he came for that purpose—so it is with the believer's difficult experiences. The problems you face are your opportunities to discover God's plan— be it to heal, deliver, mature, or use you. The evidence that you're coming to know him through prayer is that you're pleased with his plan.

Paul, for instance, delighted to share in Christ's sufferings. Unlike Paul, do you tend to beg and plead with the Lord as though he's either stubborn, ill-tempered, or disinterested? Do you try to educate him by repeatedly expressing the problem, coupled with repeated explanations of how he should solve it? Do you think he's unlearned?

Many believers lose patience with the divine process and lean heavily upon simply invoking Jesus' name in their circumstances to gain desired results. It's as though they can dispense their own answers and be wise enough to speak the right solution in every situation. Jesus' name does give access to God through prayer, but it doesn't give the right to take the scepter from his hand; that's self-deification (man's original sin problem).

The question is not, "Do you know what needs to be done?" but rather, "Do you know the Lord well enough to trust what he's doing?" Are you progressing in your relationship with him? That's God's foremost concern. Bringing you to know him properly is far more difficult than changing the circumstances of your life.

The utmost purpose of prayer, then, is to come to know God! When you face a trial, people may say, "The Lord must be trying to show you something." No! He's not trying to show you something, he's trying to show you *himself!* Trouble is a great learning center. Perhaps the disciples learned more about Christ on the storm-tossed sea than on the Mount of Transfiguration.

Battles tend to draw people closer to Christ than do blessings. The steel of saints is strengthened in the fires of affliction and shaped on the anvil of hardship. Their prayer is not so much "get me out of this" as "make me like you."

Prayer reduces the deepest hurt to no more than a passing trial and an opportunity for growth. Saints emerge from the fire having achieved the ultimate purpose of prayer—to know God better! That's his greater plan.

▪ COMMUNE WITH GOD ▪

Father, my prayers are filled with frantic efforts to get you to resolve my problems with little concern to know you as a person. Forgive me for reversing your order. Draw me to know you in such a way that when you deliver me from crisis, I don't stop knowing you. Give me eyes to see, Lord, and ears to hear how you are revealing yourself bit by bit, day by day.

■ MAKE THE TEXT YOUR OWN ■

Day One: What key thought do you wish to remember from this meditation?

Day Two: The steel of saints is strengthened in the fires of affliction and shaped on the anvil of hardship. Their prayer is not so much "get me out of this" as "make me like you." What keeps you motivated to stay faithful in prayer?

Day Three: Saints emerge from the fire having achieved the ultimate purpose of prayer—to know God better! That's God's greater plan. Have you seen that plan at work in people's lives? What historical saint do you admire as having gone through the fire and ultimately achieved God's greater plan? How do you identify with this person?

Day Four: The evidence that you're coming to know God through prayer is you're pleased with his choice. In what ways do you know God better today than before?

Day Five: You ask him for resolution; he asks you for relationship. What are you learning about God through your present trial or circumstances? What are you learning about yourself?

Of Prayer and Plots

Be . . . patient in affliction, faithful in prayer.

Romans 12:12

And we know that in all things God works for the good of those who love him.

Romans 8:28

There's never confusion before God's throne. If prayer is a mystery, it's because you're more focused on an unyielding situation than on your relationship with the Lord.

In many ways life is a mystery. But that mystery doesn't mean your life's story has no resolution. It simply means the plot is yet to unfold. Here's a fact to remember: The greater the mystery, the greater the plot.

Your time on earth is the mystery phase of your eternal existence. The story of God's grace unfolding in your life, though at times hard to see, is intended to eternally glorify him (Eph. 2:6–10). When you don't see clearly what God is doing, you struggle with his authorship, especially when the mystery thickens. Do you trust the author of your life? That will be seen in how you pray.

Before you get discouraged by the unsolvable questions that arise, remember all saints are developed through long periods, even lifetimes, of unresolved mysteries. Their maturity in sainthood is determined by the degree to which they learn to rest in the author's wisdom. They trust and pray until the final act is performed and the curtain falls. When the long night of mystery surrenders to the dawn of resolution, they enter a glory far surpassing any misery endured during the mystery (Rom. 8:18).

Why has God ordained life this way? That's not your business. Your question is simply this: Do you trust his authorship over your own, or are you always trying to take the pen from his hand in an effort to rewrite the script?

Some people become so frustrated by the mysteries they simply stop praying, leaving that to others. It's in the midst of mystery, however, that you must obey Christ's command more than ever: "Men ought always to pray, and not to faint" (Luke 18:1 KJV). Your work is not to concentrate on the mystery of life so much as on the ministry of prayer.

Jesus engaged in prayer above all things. He prayed on the spur of the moment and for prolonged periods, late at night and early in the morning—and throughout the day. In short, he prayed constantly. He was committed to God's plan despite great mysteries that often bewildered his disciples.

Through prayer, the Lord victoriously stood before the Pharisees in public places, knelt before the Father in the Garden of Gethsemane, hung between heaven and earth on the cross. These were times of vast mystery resolved by his resurrection, ascension, and enthronement.

Christ triumphantly walked through the mysteries of his life, and so can you. Paul said, "In all these things we are more than conquerors" (Rom. 8:37). We are not exempt from them. Prayer gives you confidence through the mystery, not just at the end.

Prayerful people do not become prisoners of despair, despite the depth or length of the mystery in their lives (Rom. 8:37–39). Through prayer they know the one who eventually turns things meant for harm into good (Gen. 50:20; Rom. 8:28–29).

When you pray, then, address the one who knows no confusion, since he sees the beginning from the end. By prayer, you can walk with clarity of heart even before clarity of sight. Eventually your faith will become sight when the Lord lifts the curtain on the final scene, his grand resolution to the mysteries he chose to lead you through.

▪ COMMUNE WITH GOD ▪

Father, help me to leave the pen in your hand even when I don't like the script you're writing for my life. Grant to me the trust that you're crafting a plot exceeding any I could imagine or design. Help me to see each day as simply a page—but one where something life-changing could happen—in a work much larger. Thank you for your direction and patience in the process.

■ MAKE THE TEXT YOUR OWN ■

Day One: What key thought do you wish to remember from this meditation?

Day Two: There's never confusion before God's throne. If prayer is a mystery, it's because you're more focused on an unyielding situation than on your relationship with the Lord. In what ways do you realize that your attitude toward your circumstances hinders your relationship with Christ?

Day Three: Do you trust God's authorship over your own, or are you always trying to take the pen from his hand in an effort to rewrite the script? Identify areas where you've tried to write the script.

Day Four: Prayerful people do not become prisoners of despair. What area in your life at times seems hopeless? What truth in this week's devotional gives you hope? How will you remember that truth when times get tough?

Day Five: Through prayer, prayerful people know the one who eventually turns things meant for harm into good. Read Genesis 50:20. What good came out of Joseph's sufferings? Read Romans 8:28–29. What good is being accomplished in your life?

WEEK 7 TO ENRICHMENT

Unbound
by Time

Be alert and always keep on praying.

Ephesians 6:18

Hope deferred makes the heart sick," according to Proverbs 13:12. Prayer can be discouraging when answers are long in coming. People of prayer, however, resolve to let God be the keeper of the clock.

Think how long Jesus has waited for an answer to his prayer for the oneness of the body (John 17). Certainly the mystical union is here now, but the practical union is yet to come, and the fulfillment of that prayer has been two thousand years in the making.

Other prayers have endured centuries, even millennia, awaiting their answers: prayers for the peace of Jerusalem, for Israel's return to her homeland, and for the coming of the Messiah.

It's your impulsive immaturity that gets impatient with God. You may attempt to coerce him by threatening to stop praying. But then you're the loser, not God. He'll find someone else to pray, wait, and win the reward.

When you stop praying because you've grown weary waiting for the answer, you imply that you're kinder than God *(if I were God, I'd answer this immediately)*, smarter than God *(if I were God, I'd answer it in this particular way)*, or greater than God *(I have the right to be angry with God)*. You dare to rush impetuously before God, demanding answers now! Only grace lets you survive such behavior. The delays test not God's faithfulness, but your own.

It's God who brings real solutions—in *his* time. Satan, on the other hand, promises immediate solutions, but at a price. When Jesus was in the desert, Satan offered him three quick-fixes to suffering: selfism (get yourself out of this problem by turning the stone into bread), survivalism (jump off of the pinnacle and force God to save you now), and satanism (bow to me, and I'll give you what you want, Matt. 4:3–9).

Jesus preferred, as did Job, death over disobedience. Having learned obedience by what he suffered (Heb. 5:8), Jesus later overcame Satan's effort to turn him away from the cross in the Garden of Gethsemane. The pressure was so great in the garden that blood—mingled with water—burst forth from his pores. What do we find Jesus doing during such a time? Praying!

Jesus lived thirty-three short years by lifting up prayers, some of which are taking more than two thousand years to be answered. Still, they will all be answered.

Oswald Chambers wrote that Jesus never spoke of unanswered prayer. By faith, saints pray all the time. In faithfulness, God answers all the time, but only in his time!

Jesus said, "And will not God bring about justice for his chosen ones, who cry out to him day and night? Will he keep putting them off? I tell you, he will see that they get justice, and quickly" (Luke 18:7–8).

Remember that according to the divine clock, one day is as a thousand years, and a thousand years as a day (2 Peter 3:8). Pray with all confidence, knowing that God's answer will not be one minute too early or too late.

■ COMMUNE WITH GOD ■

Father, as I wait for answers to prayer, help me not to keep an eye on the clock, but a steadfast gaze upon your throne. Know, Lord, I want to grow in trust and belief that you hear me and work the good—in good time—for me. Thank you for such love, such care.

■ MAKE THE TEXT YOUR OWN ■

Day One: What key thought do you wish to remember from this meditation?

Day Two: The delays don't test God's faithfulness, but your own. What prayer requests seem to be delayed by God's not answering? Why do you feel it's important that you receive your answer now?

Day Three: It's God who brings real solutions—in his time. Satan, on the other hand, promises immediate solutions, but at a price. If you don't wait on God to answer, what consequences might you face by trying the quick-fix methods that Satan offers?

Day Four: Why do you think Oswald Chambers wrote that Jesus never spoke of unanswered prayer?

Day Five: In light of eternity, how do you see delays to your prayer fitting into the scheme of the kingdom?

When Two Hearts Meet in Prayer

Come, let us bow down in worship, let us kneel before the LORD our Maker.

Psalm 95:6

Have you ever viewed prayer as worship? Many saints don't. But worship is the highest union between God and man. Worship is specific prayer that lifts heartfelt love and praise based upon one thing alone—who God is! When you're fully focused on worship of God, life's passing struggles are not even within peripheral vision.

The opposite of worship is worry. Despite common belief, worry isn't normal. In fact, it's an abnormality resulting from a lack of worship. Worry insists that you resolve life's problems first, then honor the Creator and Savior. Worry demands that you bow to the problem, which becomes an awful act of idolatry. How so? Idolatry occurs when you give your undivided attention to problems instead of God. That's dishonorable to the Divine.

"Oh," you say, "I don't worry." All right, then, let's call in some of worry's first cousins: irritability, nervousness, sleeplessness, and anger, to name a few. With these subtle ways, everyone tends to worry. Some people even fall back to the old saying, "Why pray when you can worry?"

The next time you're tempted to worry, worship instead! Don't withhold worship until the problem ends. Worship puts life in proper order. It says to the pesky gods of this world, "Wait here. After I've worshiped my God, then I'll handle you." And handle them you will!

True worship may be one of the most elusive experiences in the believer's life. Some people need props such as a choir and a crowd for worship, because being alone feels empty. To others, props are unnecessary, and even at times a hindrance. Because worship is the deepest expression of love to God, it's often best done when alone.

The Psalms offer the richest expressions of worship ever penned. Yet they weren't written in crowded synagogues, but when the authors were alone on hilltops, exhilarated by God's glory; in valleys, betrayed by friends; and in the palace, threatened with destruction.

Worship, then, is the meeting of two hearts in prayer—yours and God's. It's the time when all of the world is made to wait outside as you enter God's throne room. Saint Augustine wrote of a "God-shaped vacuum" in the human heart. When lost in worship, the vacuum is filled with the fullness of Christ.

You must never say, "I'll worship when I get the feeling." Worship begins by intelligently and willfully honoring God for his attributes, character, acts, and ways. Great feelings often erupt during worship, although feeling must follow the lead of the mind and the will. So don't wait for a certain feeling, just worship God! That's your main purpose in life.

True worship occurs when you meet God in prayer and he is the only focus. Strangely and wonderfully, you'll discover that generally, the greatest answers in life come when you set your requests aside while you worship, consumed by his glory more than his gifts.

▪ COMMUNE WITH GOD ▪

Father, forgive me for setting worship aside in order to focus on passing events. Help me reorder my heart to worship you above all, then witness you resolve all. Help me exercise the choice to deliberately enter your gates, your presence, your heart. Thank you for being available to me, for loving me.

■ MAKE THE TEXT YOUR OWN ■

Day One: What key thought do you wish to remember from this meditation?

Day Two: Based on this week's meditation, what is "worship"? (There are several explanations.)

Day Three: What does worship do? When does it begin?

Day Four: The opposite of worship is worry. What worry consumes your thoughts? (You may wish to complete this question after taking account of your thoughts throughout the day.) What can you do to change worry to worship?

Day Five: You'll discover that the greatest answers in life come when you set your requests aside while you worship—consumed by God's glory more than his gifts. What sacrifice (such as a prayer request) will you set aside today while you worship God?

How the Ancients Prayed

O LORD, God of Abraham, Isaac and Israel, let it
be known today that you are God.

1 Kings 18:36

There's no greater source for learning how to pray than to see how the ancients prayed. Look at how they turned mighty wheels of history through prayer: Moses spared Israel from extinction (Exod. 32), Elijah defeated and destroyed Baal's prophets (1 Kings 18), and Daniel secured Israel's release from Babylon (Dan. 9).

These ancients had no advantage over you, however. Not only were they mere mortals, they were under the Old Covenant. Under the New Covenant every promise of God is sealed with "Yes!" (2 Cor. 1:18–20), so you're the one with advantage, leaving you without excuse for failure.

The ancients did display several marks of greatness. First, they interceded for unworthy people. They didn't seek the condemnation of God's law so much as the compassion of his love, often for a most rebellious and undeserving people.

Second, they prayed at great personal expense. They put their lives on the line, expending much energy in fasting with sackcloth and ashes to see answers come to pass.

Third, they prayed in the will of God. Look at the basis of Daniel's prayer for Israel's release from Babylon: "I, Daniel, understood from the Scriptures, according to the word of the LORD given to Jeremiah the prophet, that the desolation of Jerusalem would last seventy years. So I turned to the Lord God and pleaded with him in prayer and petition, in fasting, and in sackcloth and ashes" (Dan. 9:2–3). Once Daniel saw the will of God, he prayed for its fulfillment, even though he was not near the end of the seventy years.

Fourth, they prayed for God's sake, not their own. They were profoundly concerned for God's name, reputation, and glory.

Fifth, they appealed to God on the basis of his righteousness, not their own. Once Hezekiah foolishly bartered with God by recounting his own goodness. He was given fifteen more years to live, during which he ruined his previous success (Isa. 38–39). Daniel, on the other hand, prayed, "We do not make requests of you because we are righteous, but because of your great mercy" (Dan. 9:18).

While the ancients literally determined the course of Israel's history, they cannot take your place in prayer. They can only teach you how they prayed. This is your day. Imagine the history that can be made as you—one of today's saints—pray as the ancients did!

▪ COMMUNE WITH GOD ▪

Fill me, Father, with the determination to talk with you as the ancients did, laying hold of the better things. I know the New Covenant was sealed in the blood of the Lamb in order to establish your will on earth as it is in heaven. Help me, then, rest in your mercy, and know, God, how grateful I am for it—and you.

■ Make the Text Your Own ■

Day One: What key thought do you wish to remember from this meditation?

Day Two: Read Moses' prayer in Exodus 32:7–14, 30–35. Who was Moses interceding for? Who are you interceding for today? Why?

Day Three: Read 1 Kings 18:30–39. Why do you suppose Elijah was so confident that God would answer his prayer? How can you be confident God will answer your prayers?

Day Four: Read Daniel 9. How does Daniel seek the Lord through prayer? How can you use his example in your own prayer life?

Day Five: Read 1 Samuel 23:1–6. What battles or situations are you committing to the Lord today in prayer?

Jesus: Name Above All Names

That at the name of Jesus every knee should bow.

Philippians 2:10

*A*ll prayer is lifted on the basis of a name that is assumed to be greater than the one praying. It may be a pagan calling to Baal or Zeus, a satanist calling upon Lucifer, or an Israelite calling upon Jehovah.

The great contest consists, then, in whose name reigns supreme, gains entrance into heaven, and commands the attention of the universe.

In the Old Testament the highest name of authority was Jehovah *(Yahweh)*. Then came Jesus, who established the New Covenant. All authority from Jehovah was bestowed upon Jesus (Matt. 28:18). Thus, Jesus' name now holds the highest of all divine authority.

Joseph was told to name his son Jesus (translates "the Lord saves") because Jesus would save his people from their sins (Matt. 1:21). Jesus proved himself to be the Son of God, the Savior of the world.

Every name has meaning. It may be either good or bad. When people say your name, others may respond, "There's a good person," or, "That person is untrustworthy." Because Christ proved himself worthy, God placed all authority of the universe in his name: "Therefore God exalted him to the highest place and gave him the name that is above every name, that at the name of Jesus every knee should bow, in heaven and on earth and under the earth, and every tongue confess that Jesus Christ is Lord, to the glory of God the Father" (Phil. 2:9–11).

At the name of Jesus heaven falls silent and listens, demons tremble and flee, and mountains obey and move. Jesus' name isn't to be used like a magic wand for personal success, however. It's to be used with reverence. Those who use it for any purpose other than to establish God's will in heaven and on earth (Matt. 6:10) will find themselves among the deceived, cast into the Lake of Fire (Matt. 7:15–23).

But rejoice in the prospects of properly using Jesus' name. After healing a crippled beggar by the power of Jesus' name, Peter and John advanced the gospel of salvation. Standing before the Sanhedrin, Peter said, "Salvation is found in no one else, for there is no other name under heaven given to men by which we must be saved" (Acts 4:12).

The main purpose of this highest of all names is to bring salvation. When the salvation of all people isn't central to your prayers, you misuse Jesus' name. Many great confusions have come upon the church today resulting from the improper uses of his name. But all personal blessings, from healing to finances, are incidental to salvation.

In Jesus' name is all the power and authority needed to advance the kingdom of God against the kingdom of darkness. That's done most effectively when you bathe the preaching of God's Word in prayer.

Jesus has given you the authority to use his name! This gives you the authority to prayerfully break Satan's works, and permanently advance Christ's kingdom.

■ COMMUNE WITH GOD ■

Father, you've entrusted me with the ultimate of authority,
the name of your Son, Jesus. Enable me not to sin against
you through either the misuse or neglect of this name. May I
never lose a sense of how this awesome name commands
your full attention every time it passes my lips.

■ MAKE THE TEXT YOUR OWN ■

Day One: What key thought do you wish to remember from this meditation?

Day Two: When people say your name, others may respond "There's a good person," or, "That person is untrustworthy." What does the name "Jesus" mean to you?

Day Three: In Jesus' name is all the power and authority needed to advance the kingdom of God against the kingdom of darkness. In what practical ways can you assist the advancement of God's kingdom?

Day Four: Jesus has given you the authority to use his name! This gives you the authority to prayerfully break Satan's works, and permanently advance Christ's kingdom. As you pray today, over whom will you prayerfully raise the name of Jesus to break Satan's work?

Day Five: The main purpose of Jesus' name—the highest of all names—is to bring salvation. For whom are you praying for salvation? Is there someone you want to add to your list?

Purity on the Mount

Who may ascend the hill of the LORD?
    Who may stand in his holy place?
He who has clean hands and a pure heart,
    who does not lift up his soul to an idol
    or swear by what is false.

                    Psalm 24:3–4

To be pure both by position and in practice is important to your prayer life. Think not that you can rush into heaven's throne room with dirty hands. Think not that the Holy Spirit delights to live in an unclean heart. How, then, do you gain this kind of purity?

You've already been made pure by position through Christ's obedience on the cross. You must become pure in practice by your obedience to him.

This is just the point where many people faint. They think it's too difficult to be pure in practice. But frankly, purity is more than hard. It's impossible. David knew he couldn't succeed on his own, so he asked God to create in him a pure heart (Ps. 51:10). This prayer initiates a brutal process in the refining fires of God. The heat brings death to the control of the sinful nature. That's the divine work of sanctification.

The cross, then, makes you pure by position, whereas the fire makes you pure in practice.

David spelled it out in Psalm 51:5–6: "Surely I was sinful at birth, sinful from the time my mother conceived me. Surely you desire truth in the inner parts; you teach me wisdom in the inmost place."

Knowing he couldn't muster up purity within himself, in verse 7 David asked for the fire: "Cleanse me with hyssop, and I will be clean; wash me, and I will be whiter than snow."

How can you be pure enough to climb to the highest peak on the mountain of prayer? How can you stand before God and expect the Ancient of Days to let you whisper into his ear? How can you hope for great answers?

First, confession. Confession means agreeing with God against yourself. The result? He will cleanse you (1 John 1:9).

Second, repent. Throw off every weight, that is, every sin that hinders your soul from climbing (Heb. 12:1).

Third, love God's purity. Then you'll see God (Matt. 5:8) in an abiding relationship and in mighty answers to prayer, for God's power shines most brightly when enshrined in purity.

God has provided all the climbing gear you need to reach the great summit of prayer where you'll find answers when he finds purity.

■ COMMUNE WITH GOD ■

Thank you, Father, for dressing me in robes of purity through the obedience of your Son. That encourages me to invite any fire necessary to purify me in practice. I long to stand on the summit of prayer, sense the mighty wind of the Holy Spirit, and see the grand landscape of your answers. Thank you for bringing me to this place.

■ MAKE THE TEXT YOUR OWN ■

Day One: What key thought do you wish to remember from this meditation?

Day Two: As you review today's text, how do you gain purity in practice? Is there an area in your life that must be brought into obedience?

Day Three: List the attributes of God found in this week's meditation. What favorite hymns or choruses coincide with these attributes?

Day Four: Throw off every weight—every sin—that hinders your soul from climbing. Is there anything hindering your walk with Christ? Compare the loss of being hindered by weights, to the gain found in throwing them off.

Day Five: What steps of discipline does the author of Hebrews 12:1–2 exhort you to take? Why is discipline so important in our lives?

According to Your Faith

Do you believe that I am able to do this?
According to your faith will it be done to you.

Matthew 9:28–29

A tragedy drove one woman to say, "I once believed that life was order with random chaos. Now I believe it's chaos with random order." She decided order comes by chance or accident. To those of faith, however, God is the gyro amid chaos. In fact, it is God himself who is order, and who, upon command, turns chaos into order.

Faith, after all, isn't for God's benefit. It's for yours. Can you trust God in deep valleys as well as on high summits? In turbulence as well as triumph? If not, then you may stumble needlessly.

Have you ever been irritated by health food salesmen who claim that the extract from a certain leaf or bark can heal all diseases? Some religious leaders do the same with faith, posing it as the instant cure-all for every problem. Ignorantly, people follow.

"Just speak the word of faith," they say, or, "Only make positive confessions." Indeed, by faith you can dispel demons and calm seas, but only by God's power, for his purpose, in his time. Anything else won't survive the fire.

It's easy to overstate the role of faith and misuse it. In a sense that's what happened to Lucifer, who was condemned when he tried to impose his plan on God.

After his fall, Lucifer deceived Adam and Eve by promising, "You'll be like God." He deceives Christians today by saying, "You can have anything you want by wielding faith in the name of Jesus."

Don't buy it! That only wraps the original lie in religious garb.

Am I denying that the words of Jesus can move mountains by faith? Absolutely not. Sometimes faith is empowered to move a mountain. But it's done by God's power, not faith's power. Good things happen, not because of your faith, but because of his faithfulness.

Faith rests in God despite circumstances. While a mustard seed of faith can move a mountain, it takes greater faith to have a quiet heart when the mountain doesn't move. True faith, then, believes God, even when an immovable mountain is sitting upon your shoulders.

Faith is intended to build the soul before it moves the mountain. The stronger your faith, the greater the inner rest and peace, even through times of disaster, demise, or death.

Faith is like the eagle who confronts a storm by spreading mighty wings, soaring headlong into the storm, letting the howling winds lift it above the tempest, above danger's reach. The eagle places its faith in winds it has never seen, and that leads to its graceful ascent. Likewise, those who spread wings of faith in the God who cannot be seen, ascend above the storms of life.

Why hasn't God made it easier to have faith? Why has he chosen for you to live by faith in the first place? Why is it that one time the mountain moves, then next time remains stubbornly in place? Perhaps it's God's way of testing your view of faith, to see if you're using it to be in control or to trust his control.

The ultimate prayer of faith, then, is "Thy will be done"— whether the mountain moves or not. Fear and anxiety are the dubious rewards of not adequately believing God. Peace and security are the desirable rewards of true faith.

The depth of your faith, therefore, affects the condition of your heart before it affects your circumstances. Now you see more deeply what's meant by the words, "According to your faith, it will be done to you."

▪ COMMUNE WITH GOD ▪

Father, my faith reflects exactly what I believe about you. Forgive me for being so absorbed with how I'm affected by circumstance that I fail to be concerned with how you're affected. Help my unbelief. Know my love. Remind me of this moment.

■ MAKE THE TEXT YOUR OWN ■

Day One: What key thought do you wish to remember from this meditation?

Day Two: Is it possible for your faith to become centered on yourself rather than God? What's the difference between having faith in faith and having faith in God?

Day Three: What is limiting your faith today? How can you increase your faith? Write a prayer asking the Lord to increase your faith.

Day Four: The ultimate prayer of faith is "Thy will be done," whether a mountain moves or not. What concerns do you need to commit to the ultimate prayer of faith, "Thy will be done"?

Day Five: Peace and security are the desirable rewards of true faith. Who or what disrupts peace from ruling in your heart? What can you do about this disruption?

The Wisdom of Wisdom

If any of you lacks wisdom, let him ask of God, who gives to all men generously and without reproach, and it will be given to him.

James 1:5 (NASB)

Wisdom doesn't reveal the path from which it came, but blows a whisper into the soul like a soft summer breeze, quietly governing the heart, mind, and life of the one who asks for it.

So why does wisdom hold its source a mystery? Because every person must seek and find its voice through individual hard times. No one can vicariously learn wisdom by watching another. Each learns it directly from God alone, though wisdom comes to each by a different pathway.

When you ask God for wisdom, it's immediately released from his throne. But it can't arrive while you're feeling safe, or you'll demean its value and miss its arrival. So the angel of God leads you to a calamitous place where you can meet it with full recognition and full appreciation.

Perhaps you find yourself about to lose all that you cherish. You impulsively try to defend, explain, argue, or plead your case. It's futile. Wisdom whispers, "Just be quiet." Then God delivers his wisdom without your help, thus teaching you about a dimension of life previously foreign. This principle is found in Isaiah 30:15: "In repentance and rest is your salvation, in quietness and trust is your strength."

Or the angel of God may lead you into great trouble. You're anguished by your weakness. Wisdom impresses you with a new kind of strength found in Proverbs 4:23: "Above all else, guard your heart, for it is the wellspring of life."

You'll be amazed at the peace and power that come even in the midst of trouble. But God's lesson isn't over yet. The angel may now lead you into a desert, a bewildering place that's the staging area for one of wisdom's greatest lessons—the pathway to spiritual productivity as found in John 12:24: "I tell you the truth, unless a kernel of wheat falls to the ground and dies, it remains only a single seed. But if it dies, it produces many seeds." The process of dying to self is the worst desert of your life, yet that's the birthplace of fruitfulness.

Unfortunately, wisdom is often sought only after crashing—not being led—into a wilderness. Entangled and overwhelmed by problems, it's easy to feel abandoned. But you're not. Your cry for wisdom is always met with response. Listen, and you will recognize wisdom's voice; its gentle whisper will become the firmest command of your soul.

When you emerge from the wilderness, you won't know the path by which wisdom came to you from God. All you'll know is that he brought you safely through. When others ask you to give them advice, you'll start by sending them to the throne of God.

Wisdom is careful, then, not to draw a believer to itself, but rather to God who sent it. Such is the wisdom of wisdom!

▪ COMMUNE WITH GOD ▪

Father, forgive me for thinking my common sense is the same as your wisdom. Thank you for imposing times when my natural resources fail and I'm driven to seek you alone. Thank you for responding by sending your wisdom into my wildernesses in order to lead me out.

■ Make the Text Your Own ■

Day One: What key thought do you wish to remember from this meditation?

Day Two: According to this meditation, how does wisdom come after you've asked God for it?

Day Three: In what situations have you asked for wisdom and seen God respond?

Day Four: If you were asked what the difference is between wisdom and common sense, how would you respond?

Day Five: Write down some of wisdom's characteristics described in Proverbs 2.

Asking for Trouble

I counsel you to buy from me gold refined in the fire, so you can become rich; and white clothes to wear.

Revelation 3:18

How freely may God paint a portrait of his Son on the canvas of your heart? How abundantly can God grow the fruit of his Holy Spirit in the soil of your soul? The answer to these two questions is a true measure of your spiritual depth.

Whoever dreamed of buying trouble from God by literally asking for it in prayer? "After all," you may say, "life has enough trouble without asking for more." True. But think of asking for trouble that's carefully designed by God to equip you with eternal wealth and beauty. That's what Jesus counseled the Laodicean church to do. Trouble coming to you from the vile hand of Satan is fearsome, from the unfair hand of man is formidable, but from the loving hand of God is fortunate!

Every believer should feel these burning concerns: How much do I appear like Christ? How freely does his character flow through me? Is trouble worth the trouble?

Ask God to wisely select the trouble that will form you into a masterpiece of heaven, in both the likeness and productivity of Christ.

Then read your Bible. The characters you remember best are the ones who passed through great trouble, emerged with the likeness of God, and bore the fruit of faith. These heroes of heaven became venerable giants of greatness on earth—all of them planted in the fruitfulness of God amid trouble.

For instance, how do you suppose Paul was changed from a murderous, coldhearted zealot (coldhearted toward people, zealous toward God—a dangerous combination) into the man who wrote the greatest text on love ever penned (1 Corinthians 13)? Suffering! Paul expressed strong desire to share in Christ's suffering, and suffering shaped the heart that guided the pen that amazed the world.

When you trust God to paint the likeness of his Son upon your heart, and to produce the fruit of his character in you, the world receives a harvest of goodness by which it's undeservingly blessed.

So, pray, and don't be surprised by trouble. Cast an eye on God's workmanship (Eph. 2:10). Trouble acts as both his paintbrush and plow, bringing beauty and productivity. So, why not pray fearlessly? To enter into Christ's likeness and fruitfulness is costly to you, but well worth the trouble!

■ COMMUNE WITH GOD ■

Father, I fear trouble, and rightly so if it's the kind I have brought upon myself. Remove from me all fear of asking you for trouble. I want the kind that will produce fruit which lasts forever.

■ Make the Text Your Own ■

Day One: What key thought do you wish to remember from this meditation?

Day Two: What is God's primary concern for your life?

Day Three: How has previous trouble in your life made you more Christ-like?

Day Four: Pray for trouble, with an eye cast on the beauty and wealth that only God can create, something honorable (as Eph. 2:10 says) of his workmanship. In what areas are you hesitant to pray for trouble?

Day Five: Trouble is painful, but acts as God's cleansing, refining agent. What areas of your life might seem profitable for God to send trouble in order for you to become more Christ-like?

Kingdom Praying

But seek ye first the kingdom of God, and his righteousness; and all these things shall be added unto you.

Matthew 6:33 (KJV)

Jesus taught you to live primarily concerned about the kingdom of God. Should this not, then, be the central interest of your prayers? When you put God's kingdom first, he promises to add on by meeting your needs. But many foolishly tend to reverse that order, then wonder why life gets jumbled. Do you live and pray for the add-on things first, even at the neglect of God's kingdom concerns?

If you live for the temporal add-on items, you'll move from consecration to craving, and never know great power in prayer. In essence you set yourself up as the central feature of creation with God as a bellboy, expected to respond to your every call. When he doesn't seem to answer, you say, "There, see? Prayer doesn't work." When God does grant a request, you may give him an extra tip in the offering.

Remember: What you pray to possess will possess you.

If you pray for add-on items, material things will possess you. If you pray for the kingdom, the kingdom will possess you. Jesus said, "For what shall it profit a man, if he shall gain the whole world, and lose his own soul?" (Mark 8:36 KJV).

Is your prayer centered on the affairs of the kingdom? For what, then, should you be praying? Start with these: the peace of Jerusalem, the restoration of Israel, and the oneness of God's people.

"Ah," but you say, "what do these things have to do with my needs in the real world today?"

Everything! The promise is that if you care for God's interests, he shall care for yours.

While visiting the Holy Land, I met a young woman from Pennsylvania who was there to engage in a forty-day fast for the return of Christ. Of all the things she could use her time and resources to pray for, she chose this! She had arrived in Jerusalem completely ignorant of the dangers. The cab driver wouldn't even go into the neighborhood inside Zion's Gate to drop her off at her hotel. She would have walked into the lions' den, alone, except that God had planted me in the same cab. With travel experience in Israel, I was able to offer protection and intercede for her accommodations. I have no doubt that there were a thousand other temporal needs beyond these that God surely met.

You may wonder why you should pray for something God has already said will happen, like this woman who was praying for Christ's return. You should, because that's the way God has chosen to work.

We dare not take lightly the way Jesus taught us to pray: "Thy kingdom come" (Matt. 6:10). Focus on kingdom praying, not add-on praying. God will add on the add-ons!

▪ COMMUNE WITH GOD ▪

Father, deliver me from trying to reverse your order. Enable me to believe that there's no temporal desire you cannot fulfill when I place your kingdom first. Lord, help me to love the kingdom more than its derivatives.

■ MAKE THE TEXT YOUR OWN ■

Day One: What key thought do you wish to remember from this meditation?

Day Two: How can you best rearrange or reword your prayer requests in order to align them with Matthew 6:33?

Day Three: What are some of God's kingdom concerns?

Day Four: What you pray to possess will possess you. What possessions do you feel may be binding your time and interests?

Day Five: In what new ways do you desire to focus on God's kingdom rather than on immediate needs?

Appealing to God's Grace Alone

The Pharisee stood up and prayed about himself.

Luke 18:11

*N*ever present your goodness as a bargaining chip when appealing to God. If you say, "God, look how good I've been," you only prove your ignorance of both God and yourself. The Pharisee in Luke appealed to God on the basis of his own righteousness. Since he hadn't sinned like others, he felt exalted, as though he was due privileged acceptance on high.

In contrast, the sinner dared not look upward toward heaven when he prayed (Luke 18:13). Was this self-abasement? No! He humbly understood reality. Perhaps he, like the Pharisee, had not committed gross acts of sin, or perhaps he had, but he understood the great offense of the human heart—self-exaltation. The ultimate sin is "I will make myself like the Most High" (Isa. 14:14).

How close to reality are you? That will be seen in what you offer to God to gain answered prayer. To offer your goodness implies you're trying to match his holiness with your own. That's offensive to God. Beyond offense, it's ludicrous.

David had a new view of himself following his tragic night with Bathsheba. He saw the futility of offering to God anything of himself, such as his goodness or sacrifices. Not even the blood of bulls could atone for his sin. Why? Because bulls were a lesser creation.

David lifts to God the only credible thing, the only acceptable thing, a broken and contrite heart. In Psalm 51:17, he confesses, "The sacrifices of God are a broken spirit; a broken and contrite heart, O God, you will not despise."

David's appeal is in line with reality, the realization of his sinfulness and of God's faithfulness. Animal sacrifices were only outward declarations of an inner awareness of sinfulness: "For I know my transgressions, and my sin is always before me. Surely I was sinful at birth, sinful from the time my mother conceived me" (Ps. 51:3, 5).

Said another way by the hymnwriter, "Nothing in my hands I bring, simply to thy cross I cling."

A Pharisee despises such talk, feeling it devalues him. He fantasizes that he can appeal to God upon an inherent goodness. But a humble, contrite man sees goodness as reasonable service that does not earn special advantage with God.

It's to people who face the reality of their sinfulness and humbly appeal to God's grace alone that he entrusts great answers. Great exaltations do come, however: "Humble yourselves, therefore, under God's mighty hand, that he may lift you up in due time" (1 Peter 5:6). God created mankind to be the most exalted part of creation. He can only restore that position when it is understood by mankind that such restoration is based upon grace alone.

Self-acclaimed goodness, then, is self-acclaimed glory. Such creature arrogance will not be heard on high. Conversely, God-honored goodness and grace capture the ear and heart of God.

■ COMMUNE WITH GOD ■

Father, I'm grateful that you've made me to be the highest of all creation. Forgive me when that position distorts my vision and I expect things as a result of my goodness rather than your grace. Help me to rest in your mercy, knowing you love me as I am, mistakes, depravity, imperfection, and all.

■ MAKE THE TEXT YOUR OWN ■

Day One: What key thought do you wish to remember from this meditation?

Day Two: To what do you cling as you enter God's throne room in prayer? Or what is your bargaining chip when appealing to God?

Day Three: In your own words, describe a "broken and contrite heart."

Day Four: In what area of your life might you be tempted to admit self-acclaimed goodness?

Day Five: Read Ephesians 2:8–9 and Romans 5:20–6:23. What is grace? (You may wish to check a dictionary or concordance.)

When Many People Pray

May they be brought to complete unity to let the world know that you sent me and have loved them.

John 17:23

Have you ever wondered why there are such things as prayer chains? Should you join one? Do you wonder if God hears and answers an individual's prayers? Consider the way God answered Daniel's prayer in the lions' den, David's prayer before the Philistines, and Elijah's prayer on Mount Carmel. There were no prayer chains in those places, just lonely souls crying out to their God.

At first glance it appears as though bombarding God's throne with a large wave of humanity helps get special response, much like a mass demonstration in the nation's capital. It might seem like an individual doesn't have the same strength of voice as a group. It could appear as though God bows more to public opinion than the heart-cry of one person.

Not so. God hears and responds to the bleating of one lost sheep. But there is also a divine purpose in united prayer. When a multitude comes before God's throne prayerfully focused on a need, he sees the one thing that pleases him most: Unity! Oneness!

Of course, it is dishonorable that we unite more quickly over a crisis than around the cross. But, at least for a brief moment, Christ's body behaves as one when people form a prayer chain.

The spiritual fulfillment of Jesus' prayer for the oneness of his people (John 17) came through his death and resurrection. The practical fulfillment tends to happen during a crisis. Perhaps this is one reason why God both allows and even brings crises in our lives.

Until we're prayerfully united through a crisis, pride divides us in style of worship, doctrinal variations, and cultural tastes.

But crisis, like a London fog, rolls over every wall and into every palace. No one's religious slant guarantees safety. We hear the desperate call for help all the way from the Presbyterian church to the Pentecostal, and everyone in between. Pride is crushed by a need, and we unite in prayer. We come before God in all our variations, some shouting, some crying, some lifting hands, but all united in heart over one thing.

Isn't it conceivable that the end of such united prayer can often be sad for God? After he responds, and the massive wave of prayer ends, we divide again, each to our individual traditions, sometimes with the arrogant assumption that it was one particular style of prayer above all others that got God's attention.

It was, in fact, the finished work of his Son on the cross that got his attention. But, for at least one moment in time, crisis drew us close to God's agenda of becoming one.

■ COMMUNE WITH GOD ■

Father, it's frightening to realize that I can become competitive even in prayer, and thereby divide your people. Help me bring true humility into the arena of prayer, that your house may be a place of prayer for all people, together or one at a time.

■ Make the Text Your Own ■

Day One: What key thought do you wish to remember from this meditation?

Day Two: What is the divine purpose for united prayer? In what ways have you seen God respond to united prayer?

Day Three: What is the main focus of Christ's prayer in John 17?

Day Four: What gets God's attention in prayer? What steps can you take in joining others in prayer?

Day Five: What story in the Bible reinforces the importance of people uniting in prayer for a specific purpose?

When God Hears and Answers Prayer

Before they call I will answer.

Isaiah 65:24

Crisis strikes. Instinctively you pray. That's good. But have you ever evaluated how you pray? Perhaps you begin with extensive explanations to help God thoroughly understand your situation. That may be followed by marvelous scenarios for resolution. But if your solutions are so neatly and intelligently packaged, why does God seem to have such a hard time figuring out what to do?

The fact is that he saw the problem, heard your prayer, and answered—all in eternity past. Believe it or not, he's not in search of advisors, but rather followers; those who aren't trying to give him a clue, but trusting that all is according to his purpose and plan.

So, then, why pray? Can you change anything? No, certainly not God's mind. Prayer is intended to establish his will, not determine it. Jesus clearly taught you to pray, "Your will be done on earth as it is in heaven" (Matt. 6:10). Prayer brings God's eternal plan to bear upon the present.

You must break out of the thought that God is stumbling along from event to event and crisis to crisis trying to figure out what to do. Such would be a dangerously incompetent God. Instead, you must pray with the assurance that God prepared for your sudden crisis in eternity past.

Yet you may question why you should pray. Do you still wonder, *What's the purpose?*

Picture it this way. A multi-ton ship filled with precious cargo may slide into New York's harbor from the other side of the ocean, but it still needs one little person to grab a rope and tie it to the dock. Without this person the captain cannot enter port and the supply will never arrive. Prayer is much like the dockworker's job. A sovereign ship filled with answers to prayer slides effortlessly out of eternity past. God knows from eternity past whether to send a passenger ship filled with just the right people, a cargo ship filled with just the right supplies, or a battleship filled with just the right weaponry. It's the praying person who grasps the rope and attaches the will of God to the dock.

Does God need you to pray? No. But he exalted you to this high work when he planted his image in you. He chose you as his coworker by grace. The captain and the dockworker labor in unison to accomplish the task. So prayer isn't a matter of pulling God into your panic. It's boldly, confidently fastening his eternal plan to your problem.

Why isn't it as easy as it sounds? Because you generally cry out to God while on the edge of a storm-tossed sea, or worse still, while sinking in its tumultuous depths. The fierce winds and crashing waves blind you to the reality that just beyond the temporal horizon the ship is coming!

Herein lies the work of faith that is rooted in good theology. Faith enables you to stand amid the tempest as a calm, quiet, confident, resolved believer. The most valued person is the one who grabs the rope and fastens God's eternal plans in heaven on earth's temporal shore today.

■ COMMUNE WITH GOD ■

Be delighted, O God, because when your ship filled with answers arrives at the dock, I'll be there faithfully fastening the rope by prayer. But help me to be faithful in prayer long before the ship crosses the dark horizon. O Father, thank you for this lifeline to you, too.

■ MAKE THE TEXT YOUR OWN ■

Day One: What key thought do you wish to remember from this meditation?

Day Two: When did God prepare for a sudden crisis in your life? When did God respond to your problems?

Day Three: Why should you pray if God already knows all things?

Day Four: Herein lies the work of faith that is rooted in good theology. From what source do you receive faith and good theology? What changes might you wish to make in order to devote more time to developing faith and good theology?

Day Five: How are you challenged in thinking about God's omniscience (his all-knowing character) in contrast to your limited knowledge?

Moving the Hand of God

God has surely listened and heard my voice in prayer.

Psalm 66:19

What can move the hand of God? The eruptive force of a volcano? The mighty clash of thunder? The frightening flash of lightning?

None of these can move God's hand. It's his hand that moves them. Only one thing can move the hand of God: your voice heard on high. Indeed, you move God's hand because you move his heart. You're his child cleansed by his blood, purified by his pardon, and robed in his righteousness.

Your voice calling, "Abba, Daddy," reaches heaven, penetrates his heart, and moves his hand. You're the bearer of his name. But what causes you to grow cold and pull away from this grace? Hurt? Confusion? Unfairness? Injustice? Betrayal? Temptation? When the glacier of your heart melts and you can't keep repentant tears from overflowing the walls of your soul, you'll find that the coldness wasn't the withdrawal of his arms from you, but yours from him.

Perhaps you don't feel cold, just unaccepted. What caused this? Abuse? Rejection? Fear? Self-doubt? Sin? God doesn't inflict such wounds. Rather, Christ breaks their power and heals their pain. Because you're his child, they may hurt, but they cannot harm you. So let pain drive you closer to God's throne.

Little did the blind man know, when he felt fingers rubbing mud on his eyes (Luke 9:1–7), that it was the hand of God healing him—surely an answer to many years of prayer. Think, too, of Peter's escape from the boiling waves on the Sea of Galilee, when he grasped the sea-walker's hand—yes, the hand of God (Matt. 14:25–31). There were also mothers, who had beseeched God in prayer, only to see Jesus draw their children to his lap (Mark 10:13–16). Once again, the hand of God.

So don't stop praying until you know the touch of God's hand lifting, leading, laboring—all on your behalf. Let nothing keep your voice from being heard on high. When you pray, you don't talk God into things. You establish his good gifts upon earth: "Every good and perfect gift is from above, coming down from the Father of the heavenly lights, who does not change like shifting shadows" (James 1:17).

Although your voice may never be heard by powerful people on earth, it's heard by the Almighty on high. Your voice affects the course of world events—yes, we dare say, even eternal events. Be not silent. There's no voice as powerful as the one lifted in prayer, moving the hand of God.

◾ COMMUNE WITH GOD ◾

Father, may I never be silent but vigilant in prayer. Thank you that my life matters to you, and that my voice makes a difference.

■ MAKE THE TEXT YOUR OWN ■

Day One: What key thought do you wish to remember from this meditation?

Day Two: What doesn't move God's hand? What does move God's hand? How does this encourage you?

Day Three: What causes you to grow cold and pull away from God's grace? Hurt? Confusion? Unfairness? Injustice? Betrayal? Temptation? Explain.

Day Four: Perhaps you don't feel cold, just unaccepted. What caused this? Abuse? Rejection? Fear? Self-Doubt? Sin? Explain.

Day Five: Did you ever think how it must displease the Lord when you criticize the way he made you? Use Psalm 139 as a prayer of wonder and praise as you thank God for making you just the way you are.

The Throne of Grace

Let us then approach the throne of grace with confidence, so that we may receive mercy and find grace to help us in our time of need.

Hebrews 4:16

The glory of a throne is not determined by its appearance but by the character of the one sitting upon it. In the musical *The King and I*, based upon a true story, everyone who approaches the king of Siam must remain lower than him or be killed. There's nothing new about that. Many are the stories of despotic kings who used and abused their people, holding them under a reign of fear.

Not so with our mighty God. He takes no pleasure in seeing people grovel before his throne. Grace is his disposition, extending kindness toward all who come to him. To willingly lie prostrate in honor, worship, and submission only reveals your uprightness.

Never has anyone except Christ our High Priest been worthy to approach God's throne through his own merit. No one else can approach God, saying, "I'm your equal in righteousness." The most noble of our acts are turned into filthy rags by selfish motivations.

Self-condemned, then, you come before God's throne. Your only hope is grace. And that's just what you find: Grace that receives you in Christ, makes you worthy in Christ, and declares you holy and blameless in Christ. You have no need that this grace won't meet.

Having been made holy through Christ, you're invited higher still—raised up to sit as a coequal heir with Jesus Christ in the heavenly realms. Only divine grace grants that. No earthly leader ever made you an equal heir to his throne. Having been seated upon a throne by grace, you must in turn be as the one who placed you there: full of grace!

Now with boldness you address God about your need. You're free to pour out your heart, opening the hurts and fears that reside in your deepest being. Don't fear that God will laughingly treat your need lightly. Only human cruelty does that. Even if you're getting a deserved consequence for a sinful action, God doesn't laugh. Instead, his mercy removes what you deserve so that his grace can give you what you don't—his gracious help!

Once you've come before God's throne of grace, it's incumbent upon you to take his grace with you wherever you go. You receive it to take it, and you take it to give it. When you do, you'll find upon returning to the throne that his grace is extended to you even more abundantly. The English poet Samuel Taylor Coleridge wrote, "Trample not on any, there may be some work of grace there that thou knowest not of."

God's grace is like the very air by which you live, filling your lungs, sustaining your life whether you're aware of it or not. God gives the gracious help you need either by resolving your problem or empowering you to endure and transcend it. Either way, you receive God's promised help by grace. Come boldly now.

▪ COMMUNE WITH GOD ▪

Father, you've made me worthy in Christ to come before you, fearless of ever being turned away. Help me to live worthy of this high calling. Help me to see the grace all around me—and others—like the air we breathe and need every moment of every day.

■ MAKE THE TEXT YOUR OWN ■

Day One: What key thought do you wish to remember from this meditation?

Day Two: What does grace do?

Day Three: Where does the Bible say you are seated because of God's grace? What advantage do you have from this position?

Day Four: What should you do with God's grace? With whom might you share his grace today?

Day Five: Think of several biblical examples of how God did not rescue people from their troubles, but gave them the grace to go through their troubles. In what ways does God give you the grace you need to go through trouble?

Satan: A Robber of Grace

The accuser of our brothers . . . accuses them
before our God day and night.

Revelation 12:10

Enormous forces militate to discourage you from prayer. Prayer itself isn't difficult. It's the fighting through accusing forces on your way to the throne that's the battle. Unless you identify and overcome those forces, you can be blocked from the only true source of help, God's throne of grace.

Look at the obvious hindrance. It's been said that Satan trembles to see the weakest saints on their knees. That's true. Martin Luther wrote in his hymn "A Mighty Fortress," "One little word shall fell him." Indeed, when God speaks the word, a Jericho wall that took Satan years to build will collapse in a moment of time.

Daniel describes one such victorious scene: "As I watched, this horn was waging war against the saints and defeating them, until the Ancient of Days came and pronounced judgment in favor of the saints of the Most High, and the time came when they possessed the kingdom" (Dan. 7:21–22).

Satan's vital desire is to either discourage you or stop you before you get to God's throne; he operates in the realms you pass through on your way. Once you arrive before the throne, however, Satan is forced to fight you on your turf, the ground before the throne of grace. He knows the fight is futile. That's where you become bold, addressing the one who speaks "one little word." Then Satan's best scheme against you crumbles.

There's only one way for Satan to rob you of the grace to help in your time of need, and that's to keep you away from the throne. How does he fight you? First by trying to trap you in an emotional battle where you believe the problem is too great, that you deserve your problem and are, therefore, unworthy to ask God's help, or that it would take a miracle—and such things just don't happen. Satan also will try to keep you from knowing your throne rights by whispering: "Who do you think you are to pray? You only run to God when you're in trouble. It will take someone greater than you to be heard by God."

If that doesn't work, Satan will attempt to focus your attention on human solutions: He will make you think you can work it out on your own, or he will convince you that you need more than prayer—perhaps a counselor. Or he may tell you to simply ignore your need, just wait a while and it'll go away.

So you either rob the robber or let the robber rob you. The choice is yours. Satan is powerless to stop you from going to the throne of grace; powerless, that is, unless you listen to him. Satan's lie is, "You can't go to God."

God's promise is, "I'll give you all the grace you need."

Obviously, Satan must use all his might to keep you from the throne that can fell him with one little word. Why surrender to him? Courageously go to the throne now!

■ Commune with God ■

Help me, Father, to be so attuned to the shepherd's voice that I'm not persuaded by the growl of the wolf. I look to you, Savior, to speak the one little word that fells my enemy, that I might have freedom before your throne. I know, as Acts 17:27 tells me, that you are not far, but give me courage to reach for you.

■ MAKE THE TEXT YOUR OWN ■

Day One: What key thought do you wish to remember from this meditation?

Day Two: What generally happens when you sit down to pray? Identify the forces within and without you that prevent your getting to God's throne.

Day Three: Why does Satan tremble when he sees the weakest saints on their knees?

Day Four: Who lets Satan rob you of your throne rights? Are you letting him? Why or why not?

Day Five: Many times a predetermined strategy is all you need to resist the devil. What decision can you make today to overcome Satan's opposition when you pray?

Conscience: Stealing Grace

Let us draw near to God with a sincere heart in full assurance of faith, having our hearts sprinkled to cleanse us from a guilty conscience.

Hebrews 10:22

How many times have you tried to clear your conscience before God, only to feel guilt persist in condemning you? Do you think God will never forgive you? Truth tells you that he forgave upon your confession. His pardon is complete, but still, your soul is weighted, insisting something more is needed.

Remembering that Satan is a robber of grace, you rebuke him, asking God to force him away. If still the agony persists, what can you do?

Address your conscience. It was damaged by the fall as was every other part of your being. The fall made your conscience like a Pharisee preaching law—not mercy, grace, and forgiveness—to your soul. It raises its bony finger day and night to condemn you: "You did it! Guilty! Condemned you are! Unworthy! Disqualified! How dare you think God wants anything to do with you, you unholy violator!"

All your life you were taught to let your conscience be your guide. The implication is clear. Whatever it says must be divinely correct. So how can you ever repel its condemnations?

Here's a new thought: Let the Bible be your guide, then you guide your conscience.

Frankly, your conscience doesn't give a true assessment of your standing with God. It condemns you years after God has pardoned you. And there are always preachers who agitate it with sermons that tip the scales on the side of law over grace.

You have a tough job ahead of you: retraining your conscience to understand and accept God's love, grace, mercy, and pardon—not just his law. You must insist upon the fact that you're fully accepted by God (Heb. 9:9, 14).

"Oh, yeah?" conscience questions, "if you loved God so much you would not have committed that sin in the first place. Don't think that God will forget this one easily. No, you forfeited your throne rights this time."

Since your conscience has direct access to your emotions, its arguments are believable. So you neglect prayer, believing your conscience instead of the God who calls you to rush to his throne to find grace to help even in the latest upset in your life. Remem-

ber that the God who told you to forgive seventy times seven forgives you infinitely more times than that.

Right now, take your conscience by the scruff of the neck and
insist that it believe God's Word. Insist that it fully believe mercy
triumphs over judgment (James 2:13). Then take your conscience
with you to experience the freedom found at the throne of grace.

Pray!

Once conscience is educated about grace, it becomes a powerful builder of character. It not only encourages high character,
but acts as a watchman, warning when character is in jeopardy.
A conscience once converted and trained in the way of grace is
no longer a robber of God's promises.

■ COMMUNE WITH GOD ■

*Father, I bow down in worship of you as my guide, instead
of my conscience. Thank you for setting me free and building my character along the way.*

■ Make the Text Your Own ■

Day One: What key thought do you wish to remember from this meditation?

Day Two: What's a typical argument that your conscience uses to condemn you? Identify the lie in this argument. How might you have learned to believe this lie?

Day Three: In his book *True Spirituality,* Francis Schaeffer states, "I picture my conscience as a big black dog with enormous paws which leaps upon me, threatening to cover me with mud and devour me. But as this conscience of mine jumps upon me, after a specific sin has been dealt with on the basis of Christ's finished work, then I should turn to my conscience and say, in effect, 'Down! Be still!'" In what ways do you identify with this statement?

Day Four: What's stronger? Sin, guilt, shame, or Christ's blood? If I say, "My sin, guilt, and shame are stronger," then I am claiming to be greater than God! Over what issue does your conscience continue to yell, "Guilty"? What are you going to do about it?

Day Five: Conscience is good once it's converted and trained in the way of grace. Christ's love and truth set you free from believing the false accusations of your fallen conscience. Ask Jesus to heal the wounds that taught you to believe these false accusations. What are some things you can do to cooperate with the way the Holy Spirit is retraining your conscience?

Failure: Safe in the Arms of Grace

Where sin increased, grace increased all the more.

Romans 5:20

You're heartsick. Once again you've failed. If only it were a new area of weakness; but, no, it's that same nagging place where you failed before. Your heart reasons that God is tired of your failure. You begin to believe it's useless to pray.

Don't give up! Sin cannot become greater than God's grace. Yes, you failed. You're deeply disappointed in yourself. But don't let your heart say, "I've failed again. I'm so weak, I may as well give in to this sin. I'll never be able to overcome it. I'm such a failure that my prayers don't count anyway."

Such thinking would have cost Rahab, the harlot, her own life and the lives of her family.

The reasoning of your heart is not the same as God's reasoning. Your failure didn't cause you to fall from the arms of grace. In fact, you can't fall from grace! If that were possible, then your sin would prove greater than God's grace. That's an impossibility; to be sure!

An experience from my past reminds me of this. More than thirty years ago, I was a pastor in a small Pennsylvania town and had an urgent call from a family asking if I would take their daughter to the hospital. The girl's father had told her over and over not to go near the neighbor's dog, but the little girl wouldn't listen. She found the dog intriguing. She even thought she could be friends with it. She got too close, the dog attacked, and the results were gruesome.

The father jumped into my car, holding his screaming daughter in his arms. There were slashes across her forehead and gouges in her arms. Each time she opened her mouth to release another scream, gaping wounds opened like other mouths on her cheeks. Throughout the trip her daddy held her tightly in his arms, repeating assurances, "It's OK, baby, Daddy's got you now. Daddy's with you. You're okay. Daddy's got you now."

He didn't say, "Look, kid, I told you a thousand times not to go near that dog. What's the matter with you? How dumb can you be? I cannot forgive you anymore; in fact, this time I'm disowning you. I don't want you around anymore." No, the child's disobedience had brought on a terrible consequence, but nothing in the father's heart had changed. Her failure only revealed the greater depth of her father's compassion. She was being rushed to the hospital wrapped in the arms of grace.

So it is with you and God. When you fail, God's arms of grace enfold you during the failure, not just after. Don't let failure encourage a further surrender to sin. I'm sure the little girl gave up her intrigue with the dog and never returned to pet it again. Still, she was assured that the weight of her sin wasn't too great for her father's arms of grace.

So, rise up and pray. Don't return to sin, but lay hold of your heavenly Father, thanking him for the depth and security of his grace, which is infinitely greater. The only thing you'll hear from God is, "It's OK, Daddy's got you now!"

■ COMMUNE WITH GOD ■

How safe I feel, Father, knowing that I'm always wrapped in your arms of grace. Make me wisely obedient to avoid sharp, teeth-bearing sins. Help me to choose your will every day and to see your enduring love for me.

■ MAKE THE TEXT YOUR OWN ■

Day One: What key thought do you wish to remember from this meditation?

Day Two: Read the account of Peter's personal failure in Mark 14:66–72. What do you think went through Peter's mind when he denied Christ? Why do you think he wept bitterly?

Day Three: Even though Peter had denied his Lord, what was Peter's response to Christ in John 21:1–8? How do you respond to God's love and grace after failure? Are you running to God's throne room and falling into his arms of grace, or standing afar in defeat and remorse?

Day Four: Read John 21:15–20, where Christ restores Peter to relationship and service. What's Christ's paramount concern and desire for Peter? And for you?

Day Five: Peter accepted Christ's forgiveness. That's key for us as well. In order to move forward, we need to accept God's forgiveness. Remember: There's no sin that can't be forgiven, or a sin so big that Christ would find you unuseable or unloveable. Read Acts 2:37–42, then describe in your own words how God used Peter following his failure.

God, Use Me

We are the clay, you are the potter.

Isaiah 64:8

Dear God, use me." Now that's a noble-sounding prayer. But take a deeper look at how that prayer reveals some potential flaws.

First, pride can lurk behind the prayer. It's possible you can be used of God while remaining independent of him. Pharaoh, for instance, was used of God, although he admittedly didn't know God. The question, then, is this: Do you want to be used in God's way, or do you want to use God? Are you hoping to be elevated to a position of honor without the surrender of your self to him?

Second, God doesn't use people, he loves people. God is committed to relationship, out of which great fruit is born (John 15:5). Only when your primary focus is on your relationship with God will he properly use you. Otherwise, like Pharaoh, being used by God will prove most undesirable.

Third, you probably have in mind just the way you want God to use you. But what if God chooses for you to demonstrate faith through a long-term crisis? Would you pray for God to use you if you knew up front that suffering was involved?

By the way, whatever gave you the idea that you need to ask to be used in the first place? Weren't you created by Christ and for Christ? Being used of God will be the natural result of your relationship with him. Many people who pray, "God, use me," are really trying to change the way in which God is using them. Perhaps they want God to use them in some grand, publicly spectacular way instead of in obscurity.

Here's a wiser way to pray: "God, draw me into such an abiding relationship with you that I can handle whatever way you choose to use me."

When you're abiding in Christ and he in you, it makes no difference whether God uses you in obscurity or fame. You're oblivious to both. You're absorbed in him, and that's all that matters. In fact, that's your end fulfillment, your wholeness—you and Christ together.

The Bible says little about most of the disciples. But did the lesser-known play less significant roles in being used of God than the well-known? Is a shrub growing on the White House lawn more important than a stalk of corn growing in an obscure field?

No. One yields beauty, the other bounty. Eternity may reveal that some of the little-known disciples planted more enduring seeds in the kingdom than the more famous ones.

So can you settle for knowing God and leave how you are to be used up to him? That's the only priority that leads to being used of God for his glory and honor. With that priority in place, God can trust you with great works, knowing that you won't be destroyed by the wrong focus.

Then you'll be useful, not used.

■ COMMUNE WITH GOD ■

Father, it's hard for me to accept the idea that birth, life, and growth come from your hand, not my efforts. Draw me, through prayer, into an ever-deepening, loving union with you, leaving you to determine how and when to use me.

■ MAKE THE TEXT YOUR OWN ■

Day One: What key thought do you wish to remember from this meditation?

Day Two: In what ways do you wish God to use you and why?

Day Three: Read John 15:1–17. What do you think the text means, "Apart from me you can do nothing"? Is there any area of your life in which you need to apply this statement?

Day Four: Read 1 John 2:24 and reread John 15:1–17. What does the word "remain" mean? In what ways do you demonstrate an abiding relationship with Christ?

Day Five: Many people who pray, "God, use me," are really try-ing to change the way in which God wants to work through them. How is God using you? How are you presently serving him in ministry? How do you want God to use you? Are you coveting any gifts that belong to someone else? Are you willing to accept your present ministry as his will for you today?

When God Says "No"

For no matter how many promises God has made, they are "Yes" in Christ.

2 Corinthians 1:20

Paralyzed by a crippling stroke at age 88, E. Stanley Jones was challenged by his own message that God is always saying yes. Later he wrote *The Divine Yes* in which he penned, "Now I must say this Divine 'Yes' through a shattering 'No' of a stroke. Now I must apply what I have been preaching through the years: That no matter what happens to us, the final result depends on how we take it."

While accepting no from God may be difficult, it's part of mature faith. Your need and God's no often meet like gladiators in an arena facing a life-and-death struggle. You know exactly what you need. You swing the sword of the Spirit, quoting verses of promise to God. Yet he says no.

It's not a small matter to keep your heart from dark, condemning conclusions about God. Anger rises up, judging God's seeming lack of love and wisdom. Frustration chokes hope. The voice of time mocks ever loudly. You're amazed at his unwillingness to act in your behalf; after all, you're praying about a serious need (perhaps one he brought to pass), not merely a shabby want of your own.

You remind God that all of his promises are yes in Christ Jesus.

Then it strikes you, the thing you've been missing. When God says no, it's always echoed by a yes. That doesn't make sense at first, but you start to reason it out. When God says, "Thou shalt not," it is followed by, "Thou shalt!"

Once you get the hang of this, it pops up everywhere in Scripture. For instance, God said no to Paul's plan to go to the region of Phrygia and Galatia (Acts 16:6–7). How frustrating. First God tells Paul to preach to the Gentiles, then blocks his way—and I mean blocks it with impassable boulders. We read, "but the Spirit of Jesus would not allow them." And that's that. *Finis!*

Paul couldn't know that a yes would follow the no. He fell asleep trusting God's no. The yes came in a vision. He saw a man from Macedonia inviting him to come and help (Acts 16:9–10). Think what would have happened if Paul had stomped his feet and pressed against (or even defied) God's no. He not only would have missed the Macedonian call, he may have found himself in a major crisis like Abraham, who nearly lost his wife (and life) when seeking refuge in Egypt.

Does your heart still recoil from a divine no as though from a venomous viper? Pride warns that you're being neglected, as though you're unimportant and insignificant. It insists that your microscopic view is the panorama of the whole universe. It demands full explanation as to why God would dare say no.

Does fear well up, perceiving no to be an end, not a bend? God doesn't make dead-end plans, only new paths obscured by present ones. You are praying earnestly about how a path should both begin and end. You present God with excellent ideas of how to do it. But God's pathways extend into eternity. Often, you won't see the end until then.

So when God says no, it's to a short-range goal with no eternal significance. When he says yes, his eternal purpose is stamped all over it.

As you pray, then, you can be sure that no will ultimately result in yes. Don't be so focused on your demand—the one to which God is saying no—that you miss the marvel of the divine yes. God said no to Joseph's natural desire for a happy home life, but said yes to using him to deliver his family, and a nation, from destruction (Gen. 37, 39–47).

How deeply do you trust God's integrity to turn a no into a yes?

■ COMMUNE WITH GOD ■

Father, help me to remember that no is not in your loving heart, unless my desire is self-destructive or outside of your perfect will. Your no is not an end, only a bend in my pathway, always leading to a yes.

■ MAKE THE TEXT YOUR OWN ■

Day One: What key thought do you wish to remember from this meditation?

Day Two: Aren't you glad that God doesn't always answer your prayers the way you hoped? Think of an example where God spared you by saying no.

Day Three: In 2 Samuel 7:1–17, what no did David receive? Even though David's desire was good, it wasn't God's perfect timing, nor was David the man for the job. What yes did David receive and who did God ordain?

Day Four: As you pray, you can be sure that no results in yes. Don't be so focused on your demand—to which God is saying no—that you miss the marvel of his divine yes. What are some possible reasons why God may be saying no to a certain prayer request? Ask him to help you see the yes in your given situation.

Day Five: T. J. Bach once said, "Where God has put a period, don't change it to a question mark." Is there any area of your life where you've not accepted God's no and are still hoping he'll change his mind? If so, why do you desire to cling to something that God knows is not in your best interest?

When God Says "Wait"

I waited patiently for the Lord; he turned to me
and heard my cry.

Psalm 40:1

Waiting on God to guide in answer to prayer has proven to be a major stumbling block for many. But to reach for something ahead of God's time, even a good thing, is a lethal violation of faith. It's hard to resist the temptation to fulfill your own prayers by your own strength and in your own time by using your own genius and resourcefulness.

The Bible is filled with stories of people who didn't wait for God. One of the most blatant examples was the king of Israel's response when Ben-Hadad laid siege on Samaria during a time of famine (2 Kings 6:24–33). Simply put, Israel was in deep trouble. The king's first response was to a desperate woman, telling her that if God didn't help her, then he certainly couldn't either. His second response was to blame Elisha for the mess, even vowing to slay him. Finally he took on the Almighty himself by saying, "This disaster is from the LORD. Why should I wait for the LORD any longer?"

Have you ever been in such a situation, disgusted with God's seeming tardiness in light of your need? It's a dangerous time, a time when the heart will reveal its true self and spew awful things before the Lord. Countless people have forged into the jungle, swinging the machete of self-will, only to find themselves hopelessly lost.

Saul was another one who insisted on getting ahead of God. His son Jonathan stirred a hornets' nest when he attacked the Philistine outpost at Geba. Their furious response caused fearful quaking among Saul's men as they awaited the appointed time for Samuel to make a burnt offering to the Lord. Then, when Samuel didn't come at the expected time, Saul made the offering himself (1 Sam. 13). What was the result of pushing the hands of God's clock? Saul lost the privilege of having his kingdom established forever. The honor went to David instead.

In the New Testament, Satan tried to persuade Jesus to deliver himself from suffering instead of waiting on God (Matt. 4:1–11). All three desert temptations were quick-fix solutions for suffering. Paraphrasing, Satan's taunting words went something like this: "Get yourself out of this mess. You have the power. Turn that stone into bread. You don't have to be hungry. If you don't want that solution, then jump off of the temple and force God to save you now. And if you really want to stop suffering and get the kingdoms of the world, bow to me."

Jesus' response was, in essence, "Absolutely not! I'll wait on God."

Prayerfully waiting on God is of the utmost importance. Waiting is a hallmark of faith: faith that God can and will deliver you, even though your trouble worsens; faith that God has not forgotten or neglected your cause, and that God's character will prove trustworthy.

Not waiting on God speaks the opposite!

To not wait on God is like picking fruit before it's ripe—a sour stomach results, if not something worse. The wise person learns to follow divine timing. Ecclesiastes 8:6 states, "For there is a proper time and procedure for every matter, though a man's misery weighs heavily upon him."

So what should you do while you wait? Should you sit and stare forlornly like a deserted child? No. You run with indefatigable confidence and walk with irrepressible hope (Isa. 40:31). Renewing strength flows from on high. The very thing that threatens you becomes threatened. Darkness retreats before light. God comes just in time. He honors you in the deliverance if you honor him in the wait.

■ COMMUNE WITH GOD ■

Father, find me among those who wait for you, be it in the desert or in the palace. Give me the strength for stillness, and know I want your will—and a heart to accept it, whether it's sooner or later.

■ MAKE THE TEXT YOUR OWN ■

Day One: What key thought do you wish to remember from this meditation?

Day Two: What prayer requests are you waiting for God to answer? How long have you waited for God to respond?

Day Three: Explain how you're certain that what you're asking for is in alignment with God's will and purpose for your life.

Day Four: James 1:5 says, "If any of you lacks wisdom, he should ask God, who gives generously." Why not spend a few moments throughout today asking God for his wisdom and perspective regarding the delay to your unanswered prayer?

Day Five: Make two columns, one headed "Foolish" and the other "Wise." Write down the traits of a foolish person and those of a wise person. How do your thoughts and actions reflect those of a wise or foolish person?

The Battle for Control

He is the Lord; let him do what is good in his eyes.

1 Samuel 3:18

Prayer is the arena in which the contest is fought over who will rule your life. Deep within your natural heart resides Satan's garden lie, "You will be as God." Spiritual maturity is determined by the depth to which you exchange the lie for this truth: "You will know that I am God."

How can you test your level of growth? By your response to life's situations. There are basically three levels of response. First, there are situations over which you have no control, things like taxes, death, and unruly people. Do you merely concede to such areas? Resign out of fatigue? Are you just too tired to fight anymore? Or are you resting comfortably by faith, knowing that God is doing all things well?

The second level is more difficult. This involves trusting God when he allows pain to be inflicted by the things over which you have no control. Does your heart thrash about, disturbed by God's apparent disinterest in your plight? It's the thrashing that reveals your demand for control. You're troubled that you don't have the ability to change those things.

The third level is the ultimate test. You consciously, intentionally give God control over areas that you could otherwise control by yourself. These include your time, abilities, resources, relationships. The battle lines are drawn over who holds the ultimate rights to rule your attitudes, actions, and decisions—in short, all of you.

The war intensifies when you pray not for new gadgets, but to know and serve God better. Too many times too many people tend to treat God as an opponent. It's possible to interpret his silence and patience in the battle for control as weakness. But don't be fooled by your opponent's seeming lack of strength. He could easily pull your arms out of their sockets and make a show of brute force. But he doesn't. He quietly, gently, patiently invites you to surrender—intelligently, willingly surrender all rights to him. He waits in kindness, politeness, meekness—the quintessence of humility.

Sometimes you yank frantically on your end of the rope, but find you can't pull him off his throne. In turn, he tugs so gently that you barely notice. He's waiting on you to discover both the foolishness and futility of Satan's lie that self-rule can work. His love and wisdom won't surrender his role of sovereignty to you.

In a real sense, then, you're at war with yourself. He waits on you to choose whom you will allow to have control. Will it be you or him? This is a recurring battle. But when you prayerfully submit, you discover why he didn't overpower you with bullish might. God doesn't desire you to be a comatose slave, but a friend like Abraham of old—a friend of God.

God is far more interested that you know him than that you serve him. It's all about relationship. After all, he's big enough to get things done with or without you. But all true, lasting accomplishments grow directly out of knowing him.

This is the abiding relationship Jesus spoke about in John 15:5. He is the vine and you are the branch. No fruit is born without this life-force coursing from the vine through the branch and to the fruit. As in a good marriage, strength comes out of oneness. All fruit comes out of your union with Christ. That union begins by surrendering all your rights to him.

Strangely, when you release control to God, you find strength given to be in control, the very thing you feared to lose.

■ COMMUNE WITH GOD ■

Father, help me to learn to release all control into your
hands and not to wrench it back. Even when you don't
seem to be in control, help me to surrender, in faith, to you.

■ MAKE THE TEXT YOUR OWN ■

Day One: What key thought do you wish to remember from this meditation?

Day Two: There are situations over which you have no control, things like taxes, death, and unruly people. What experiences in your life would fall under this category in which you may have questioned God's sovereignty?

Day Three: The second level is more difficult. This involves trusting God when he allows pain. What areas or circumstances have left you feeling like a victim, in confusion and pain?

Day Four: Amy Carmichael, a missionary to India in the early 1900s, said, "Nothing in life can harm you, only your response." How might this apply to victims of abuse, accidents, and other tragedies? How does this apply to you?

Day Five: The battle lines are drawn over who holds the ultimate rights to rule your attitudes, actions, and decisions—in short, all of you. What attitudes, actions, or decisions have you not surrendered to Christ? Why or why not?

Death of the Lie

"You will not surely die," the serpent said to the woman. "For God knows that when you eat of it your eyes will be opened, and you will be like God."

Genesis 3:4–5

What inspires you to pray? Speakers? Books? Crises? Do grand achievements through prayer flood your mind? Do you brilliantly observe problems on earth, then report them to God in heaven, or even advise him on what action to take? *How fortunate God is to have me*, you may think.

But soon after you start to pray, perhaps life begins to fall apart. Nothing goes as expected. God seems indifferent to your effort. You add some fervor to your prayers. You raise your voice, or even sweat a little. Still, a gravitational force seems to keep your prayers earthbound.

What's happening? You're being taught the first major lesson of prayer: You are not God.

You may argue that you never thought you were. The truth is you were born with Satan's garden lie (you will be as God) woven into the very fabric of your nature. It's a lie that deceives you to your face. That lie must be completely exposed and slain—literally. That slaying is a lifelong process. It's good that you've committed yourself to prayer, or your mind wouldn't be able to handle the process of killing the lie.

The depth to which the lie has been slain is seen in the depth to which you can pray as Christ did: "Not my will, but yours be done" (Luke 22:42). This is not a passive resignation to the inevitable, like a clam plundered by a wave; rather, it's an active commitment to go from your Gethsemane to your cross.

What is your Gethsemane? It's the choice to do life God's way even though everything within you seeks a way to rewrite the script. What's your cross? The ultimate cross is the death to sin; which is, in essence, death to self-rights, self-rule.

Why must there be a cross? Because all that God does comes through the cross. Christ died on Calvary's cross to remove the penalty of the lie. You die on your cross so that the lie no longer rules over you. Until then you're useless to heaven.

The depth to which the lie is still alive is seen in the intensity of the wrestling of your heart in depression, fear, rage, self-justification, or arguing. You attack whatever attacks you, rather than trust God's sovereign plan to expose and slay the lie. There's hope when, in time, these violent upheavals quiet to a murmur, then fall silent.

Finally you're dead, at least to some degree. The heart is done fighting God. There's silence. What now? The silence of death is a vacuum into which spiritual life rushes like a mighty wind. Your prayer life pulsates with meaning beyond your wildest imagination. God's wisdom acts as a bridle directing prayer. Understanding brings power where once ignorance reigned. Patience drives prayer over the long haul until the victory comes.

At last you figure it out: Prayer really does work. The same God who either caused or allowed your world to fall apart pieces it together again. God first used prayer to expose and slay the lie in you. Then he used it to fill you with power and truth. Now he's using it for grand achievements.

■ COMMUNE WITH GOD ■

Father, find me faithful through the process of the death of the lie and the resurrection of prayer. Give me the imagination to glimpse the depth of your mercy and the extent of your power.

■ MAKE THE TEXT YOUR OWN ■

Day One: What key thought do you wish to remember from this meditation?

Day Two: What or who has inspired you to become a person of prayer? Explain.

Day Three: The depth to which the lie has been slain is seen in the depth to which you can pray as Christ did: "Not my will, but yours be done." Over what issue or person are you having a tough time praying, "Not my will, but yours"? Why?

Day Four: What's your Gethsemane? It's the choice to do life God's way even though everything within you seeks a way to rewrite the script. What's your cross? The ultimate cross is the death to sin; which is, in essence, death to self-rights, self-rule. Name your Gethsemane and your cross.

Day Five: The depth to which the lie is still alive is seen in the intensity of the wrestling of your heart in depression, fear, rage, self-justification, or arguing. Do any of the responses listed here reveal that the lie of self-deity is still alive in your heart? How so?

Faith Dancing at Dawn

How long, O LORD, must I call for help,
but you do not listen?

Habakkuk 1:2

Israel is dripping with rebellion. The prophet Habakkuk is sick of it and decides to let God know just how he feels. His outburst reveals a threadbare faith. He has a belly full of injustice, watching evil people overpower and abuse good people. Railing out of raw reason, the prophet angrily confronts God for neglect and corrects God for slowness in judging Israel's sin. "Judge Israel now!" he demands.

Habakkuk has no idea that heaven's war machine (Babylon) is moments away from rolling across Israel, subjugating her under pagan power and ultimate humiliation.

Thank you, Habakkuk. Thank you for being frail in faith like me.

Thank you, God, for revealing the fragile faith of your great prophet.

Indeed, this man's faith wore thin in the face of God's seeming disregard for justice and the plight of the faithful. The prophet's bold indictment doesn't shame God into action. It just so happens that Habakkuk's prayer and God's plan bump together at the same time. God gives the prophet a chilling response: "Look at the nations and watch—and be utterly amazed. For I am going to do something in your days that you would not believe, even if you were told" (Hab. 1:5).

Habakkuk's faith awakens, at least somewhat. He calls God "Rock." Now, realizing that Israel is about to be plundered, his concern shifts. He thinks God may be going after rabbit, loaded for bear. He questions why God would use evil people to chasten the evil in Israel; after all, he sees that the Babylonians are a bunch of pagans while Israel is God's chosen nation. He's glad God is doing something, but fears God is going too far.

It's in this setting that God makes a statement that shatters the prophet's angry defenses: "But the righteous will live by his faith" (2:4). What a wake-up call. In the midst of disaster, when it appears as though God is a do-nothing sovereign, faith declares, "God, I believe you!"

The result? God declares the believer righteous (Rom. 1:16–17). All upright people emerge from crooked people by divine declaration. Their faith in God is accounted to them for righteousness. Eventually that transforms them completely.

After reminding Habakkuk to have faith in him, God firmly puts Habakkuk back in his place by saying, "The LORD is in his holy temple; let all the earth be silent before him" (Hab. 2:20). In other words, when you don't understand what God is doing, have the sense to be quiet and worship him.

Habakkuk feels the firm slap of "gentle" love. Circumstances haven't changed; in fact, they're going to get worse as Israel is on the brink of a seventy-year captivity. But Habakkuk's faith is reawakened. His countenance turns radiant because of a transformed heart. He cannot contain his jubilance.

The final chapter is like a worshipful dance in the dawn. Habakkuk writes, "His glory covered the heavens and his praise filled the earth. His splendor was like the sunrise; . . . His ways are eternal. . . . Yet I will wait patiently for the day of calamity to come on the nation invading us. . . . I will be joyful in God my Savior" (Hab. 3:3–4, 6, 16, 18).

■ COMMUNE WITH GOD ■

Father, I join Habakkuk in a worshipful dance at dawn. I cannot withhold my praise from you. You do all things well!

■ Make the Text Your Own ■

Day One: What key thought do you wish to remember from this meditation?

Day Two: According to Hebrews 3:12, what sin is revealed? Have you ever considered unbelief as sin? In what areas or concerns do you have a hard time believing God?

Day Three: Faith is the foundation of Christian character and the security of the soul. What can you do to increase your faith?

Day Four: Since joy and contentment are two measuring sticks of faith, how have you seen your faith mature over the past year?

Day Five: When you don't understand what God is doing, have the sense to be quiet and worship him. In what ways do you worship God when you simply don't understand what he's doing?

Appeasing Your Heart

You do not delight in sacrifice, or I would bring it.

Psalm 51:16

One sign of spiritual growth is that your sin will produce trauma in your heart. As you draw closer to God, even so-called small sins produce great discomfort. Your first instinct is to want to appease God, so you pray, but the disturbance remains. What's the problem? Does it take time to appease God? No. God was fully appeased when his Son paid for all your sins on the cross.

The problem is in appeasing yourself. While sin violates God, it violates you as well.

The word *appease* sounds soft, but it's a powerful word. Look at Webster's Deluxe Unabridged Dictionary (second edition) to capture the full force of the word: "Appease—to make quiet; to calm; to still; as to appease the tumult of the ocean or of the passions." Isn't that the cry of the heart needing to experience the embodiment of peace?

Webster gives some synonyms that reveal vital undercurrents of appeasement: "calm, pacify, quiet, still, allay, assuage, soothe, tranquilize—to appease is to allay agitation which demands satisfaction." No words could better describe a healthy heart.

When you sin, you lose a quiet heart. You're disturbed, so you assume God is too. Confession doesn't lift the thick, lingering heaviness. Turmoil reigns. You keep trying to appease God and hope he'll get over it. But as already mentioned, it's settled with God. You need God to help you get over it. That's done through the process of prayer.

King David had the right perspective in his repentant prayer found in Psalm 51. He opens the psalm by establishing that God has mercy and is unfailing in compassion. The problem is not with God, but with David. Most of his prayer is comprised of asking God to restore him and bring appeasement to his heart. Look at the phrases he uses:

- "For I know my transgressions, and my sin is always before me" (v. 3).
- "Cleanse me with hyssop, and I will be clean; wash me, and I will be whiter than snow" (v. 7).

- "Let me hear joy and gladness; let the bones you have crushed rejoice" (v. 8).
- "Create in me a pure heart, O God, and renew a steadfast spirit within me" (v. 10).
- "Restore to me the joy of your salvation" (v. 12).
- "O LORD, open my lips, and my mouth will declare your praise" (v. 15).

David isn't trying to appease God; rather, he is throwing himself upon a merciful, faithful, and compassionate God to bring appeasement to himself, to settle the disturbance caused by his sin. David doesn't engage in self-help psychology to talk himself out of his problem. He asks God to do a work in him that only God can do: cleanse, renew, restore, create.

The search for peace is global. But will peace be found in a bottle, a pill, or an organization? These things may bring momentary relief, but never peace. When God grants his peace, there is no psychological formula. It goes beyond understanding (Phil. 4:7).

Seek God to settle your heart, to grant you "ap-*peace*-ment." Don't get caught in the deception that suggests you must appease God. That was settled at Calvary.

Appeased, now pray.

▪ COMMUNE WITH GOD ▪

Father, I rejoice to know that you are fully appeased by the blood of your Son shed in my behalf. Now, quiet my heart by the same blood sacrifice.

■ MAKE THE TEXT YOUR OWN ■

Day One: What key thought do you wish to remember from this meditation?

Day Two: While sin violates God, it violates you as well—and it's you who needs appeasement. Over what sin or circumstance do you feel impure, violated, discouraged, or defeated? Why?

Day Three: God doesn't show favoritism (Acts 10:34). What he did for David, he will do for you. What have you done that you feel is beyond the work of Calvary? Are you ready to lay it at the foot of the cross? The choice is up to you.

Day Four: Are you ready, once and for all, to bring that disturbance in your heart to the cross of Calvary? If so, follow the steps outlined by David in Psalm 51.

Day Five: What does Romans 8:1–4 say about your relationship with Christ? Can you accept this truth for yourself?

How Disturbance Distorts Your View

Know my heart. . . . See if there is any offensive
way in me.

                              Psalm 139:23–24

While disturbance in the heart can instigate prayer, it often distorts prayer. How? Because disturbance in the heart is generally caused by a misperception of God. This is reflected in the prayers of many biblical characters:

- **Habakkuk** is angry that God doesn't intervene to stop human injustice (1:2–4).
- **Jeremiah** complains bitterly that God lets the wicked prosper (12:1).
- **Job's** nerves run thin over God's silence in the midst of his suffering (30:20).
- **David** rails that God is not beating up his enemies quickly enough (Ps. 13:1–4).

Were their disturbances understandable? Yes. Were their disturbances valid? No. Then what was the problem? Their perspective of God was wrong. Their disturbed hearts turned to praise, however, when they regained a proper view of God. Keeping a proper view of God is essential, then, to an effective prayer life.

But do life's experiences seem to conspire against your view of God? Do enemies threaten to undo you? Do physical problems reveal your fragile state? Do setbacks open the door to discouragement? Do personal inabilities and failures defeat you?

If you approach God with these disturbances in the heart, your first instinct may be to blame God for letting bad things happen. This is essentially accusing him of parental neglect. Since you can't report him to a higher authority, you fly off the handle in anger against him.

Frankly, God has heard it all from the best and, fortunately, isn't thin-skinned. It's you, however, who loses. When disturbance distorts your view of God, you dishonor God and demean yourself. Your accusatory prayers reveal the depth of your spiritual immaturity.

What was the cure for the people of the Bible? Was it an immediate correction of their problems? Rarely. Inevitably, it was the reconstruction of their view of God. This led eventually to a resolution to their problem. How can you rebuild your view of God? I've found no substitute for lengthy, quiet time spent in absorbing God's revelation of himself. That was the psalmist's solution: "I have hidden your word in my heart that I might not sin against you" (Ps. 119:11).

Martin Luther spent an average of two hours a day in meditation and prayer. When asked what he did on busy days, Luther answered, "I pray four hours."

The heart can only build its perceptions out of what it is fed. Water will never rest where the winds are steady and strong. Let the wind cease, however, and the water glazes smooth as glass. The same is true of the heart. The whipping winds of our tumultuous world will trouble any heart. Only when you are focused on the Prince of Peace will you hear him say, "Peace, be still."

In the end, heartfelt disturbance is a sin against God. Consider the things that disturb us: Jealousy says that God isn't giving you enough. Anger says that God isn't judging someone enough. Envy says that God unfairly gave another something you deserve. Greed says that if God won't give it, then you must grab it. Rage says that you must not wait on God, but fight your own battles. Impatience says that God doesn't understand the need for getting things done now.

On and on goes the list, showing how every sinful disturbance of the heart is first and foremost an indictment against God. That's serious. It diminishes your sense of the glory of God and fractures the soundness of the heart. The Bible is clear: "Above all else, guard your heart, for it is the wellspring of life" (Prov. 4:23).

So don't justify disturbance in your heart. Use it as a tool to reveal and correct a wrongful view of God. Absorb God's Word until you can say with David, "He put a new song in my mouth" (Ps. 40:3). Then you'll pray freely.

■ COMMUNE WITH GOD ■

Help me to see you in all your magnificence, Father. May my heart be quieted of all disturbance, and may praise alone flow unto you.

■ MAKE THE TEXT YOUR OWN ■

Day One: What key thought do you wish to remember from this meditation?

Day Two: In Proverbs 4:23 we are told, "Above all else, guard your heart, for it is the wellspring of life." So guarding your heart is a deliberate action, a willful choice. What steps do you need to take today to guard your heart? Write out a plan that's workable for you.

Day Three: Many times you pull God down to your view and way of thinking. How can you exalt God in your thoughts to his rightful position?

Day Four: How do you evidence that you are completely dependent upon the Lord? What evidences show that you may not be?

Day Five: With which of these statements do you identify, and how? In the end, heartfelt disturbance is a sin against God. Consider the things that disturb us. Jealousy says that God isn't giving you enough. Anger says that God isn't judging someone enough. Envy says that God unfairly gave another something you deserve. Greed says that if God won't give it, then you must grab it. Rage says that you must not wait on God, but fight your own battles. Impatience says that God doesn't understand the need for getting things done now.

Putting Right Another's Wrong

After that, God answered prayer in behalf of the land.

2 Samuel 21:14

*I*t may sound strange at first, but sometimes you have to put right another person's wrong before seeing prayer answered. I know our society is deeply inoculated with the idea that everyone is responsible for their own sin (good old-fashioned individualism). But community is as important to God as are individuals. People can pass both blessings and problems to one another.

A biblical illustration of this is Achan, whose sin cost Israel a victory at the small town of Ai (Josh. 7). Many years later a similar thing occurred in Israel because of Saul's sin. Saul, Israel's first king, had broken a peace treaty with the Gibeonites, who were descendants of the Amorites. Saul attempted genocide, intending to obliterate them from the face of the earth. The result? God plunged Israel into three years of famine (2 Sam. 21:1–2).

In time, Saul died on a battlefield, leaving his throne in shame and his nation in famine. What a dismal end. It all came to pass because he broke his word. Unfortunately, Saul's word was known to be unreliable from the start. He had launched his kingship, for instance, by not waiting for Samuel to make the opening sacrifice. Then, he broke his promise that he would not harm young David. Saul attempted repeatedly to impale him on the tip of his spear. The end of Saul's kingship was characterized by disgrace, death, and drought.

David, on the other hand, launched his kingship by putting right the wrong of another man. David asked the Gibeonites, "What shall I do for you?" They asked for seven of Saul's male descendants to be given to them for execution. David, faithful to Saul's son Jonathan, did not offer certain men of Saul's descendants. He gave only those not under a binding word. But he did give over others in an effort to make right Saul's wrong (2 Sam. 21:3–9).

So we have three scenarios of behavior: Saul's broken word resulting in national demise; the Gibeonites' vengeful spirit resulting in shaming Saul's house (interestingly, the pages of history have nothing good to say about these people); and finally, David's efforts to put right Saul's wrong, even collecting his bones, giving this dishonorable man an honorable burial. The result? The floodgates of relief are opened: "After that, God answered prayer in behalf of the land."

Possibly there's one of three things hindering your prayers. God may be developing a deeper faith, one that is tried and proven through a long, hot drought. Two, God could be chastening a sin, digging it out of a deep crevice in your heart. Or three, God may be waiting on you to put right another person's wrong—that is, if it's within your power.

Don't think that because this is an Old Testament story it doesn't apply today. The New Testament doesn't endorse individualism either. The church is as fitly framed together in complete interdependence as the muscle coordination of your body.

If you have the power to make right another person's wrong, do so! That may be the key to having the script of your life read: After that, God answered prayer.

■ COMMUNE WITH GOD ■

Reveal to me, Father, any sins committed by others that I'm able to make right: debts to be paid, regret to be expressed, restitution to be made. I want to bring about justice wherever I can so my prayers are unhindered.

■ MAKE THE TEXT YOUR OWN ■

Day One: What key thought do you wish to remember from this meditation?

Day Two: Of the following options, which do you believe may be hindering your prayers? God's developing a deeper faith, one that is tried and proven. God's chastening a sin, digging it out of a deep crevice in your heart. God's waiting on you to put right another person's wrong.

Day Three: Do you know of any of the following wrongs that could be made right in your life or that of another? The bringing of two people together who are at odds. Confronting someone who has judged you or another person wrongly. Setting some-one free by confronting them with truth.

Day Four: Are there any promises that you've made or implied to a friend, neighbor, family member, or brother or sister in Christ that you haven't honored?

Day Five: If you aren't sure how to handle what God has shown you this week, are you willing to ask him for wisdom and insight in knowing how to put your faith into action?

God Listens for Your Heartbeat

I will meditate on all your works and consider all your mighty deeds.

Psalm 77:12

Meditation doesn't always demand long hours. A hurried life isn't a shallow life provided you take deep thoughts with you throughout the day. Stop often to think on them. Sometimes one sentence can open a deep well of wisdom, for the thoughts you feed into your heart determine the condition of your soul. Fill your heart with the right meditations, and your heart fills you with confidence that your life is being invested, not expended.

Your heart's condition is as vital to prayer as the words of your mouth, and sometimes more so. It's wonderful to tell someone of your love, either with tender speech or flowing pen. But the communication of love reaches its finest moment when two hearts simply beat as one. At that time there are no words, just heartfelt unity. Unquenchable flames erupt, love is sealed, and a bond forms equal to the strength of death (Song of Songs 8:6). In fact, Solomon warns not to awaken this force until the proper time (2:7), because it's a consuming passion.

On this level of love, soul knows soul. Instinctively the two know and care for each other's hearts. This image is close to the relationship you can develop with God. The greatest commandment is to love the Lord with all your heart, soul, mind, and strength (Matt. 22:37–38). How do you develop such a union of heart with God?

Meditation!

That word "meditation" sounds mild, but it's the pathway to your deepest knowledge of God. You meditate on all that you value. People in love instinctively meditate on their relationship, and the meditation is so intense that they feel together even when apart. Likewise, to know God deeply and to love him fully demands consistent meditation.

The one thing that will kill meditation is busyness! "I'm just too busy," you say. If you view meditation on God's Word as a luxurious pastime, then you'll always believe, "I don't have time for that." That kind of attitude will lead to the destruction of any relationship. Get ruthless with anything that hinders your meditation. You can only come to know God when you say to the world around you, "I'm meditating. I don't have time to be busy."

Meditation is not only central to relationship, it's indispensable to success. One of the few times success is mentioned in the Bible is within the company of meditation. God said in Joshua 1:8, "Do not let this Book of the Law depart from your mouth; meditate on it day and night, so that you may be careful to do everything written in it. Then you will be prosperous and successful."

David described his relationship with God this way, "May the words of my mouth and the meditation of my heart be pleasing in your sight, O LORD, my Rock and my Redeemer" (Ps. 19:14). He was pleased with God and wanted to please God, and so it was that God was pleased.

When you turn your heart toward the voice of God, he turns his ear toward the beat of your heart—and this is when prayer is complete.

This kind of relationship comes through meditation alone. In *Walking on Water* Madeleine L'Engle wrote, "When there is no time for being there is no time for listening." God's most important messages are whispered into the hearts of those who, through prayer and meditation, take time to listen.

◾ COMMUNE WITH GOD ◾

*Be pleased, Father, to see that my heart turns toward you in
quiet times of meditation. I desire you above all else.
Remind me of the beauty of these quiet times during the
chaos of my day. Help me to find ever-new ways of stealing
away with you in the midst of everyday cares. I'm grateful
for your promised presence.*

■ MAKE THE TEXT YOUR OWN ■

Day One: What key thought do you wish to remember from this meditation?

Day Two: The thoughts you feed into your heart determine the condition of your soul. What issues or thoughts are consuming you today—thoughts of fantasy, worry, fear? Or are you thinking of gratitude and reflecting upon God's Word, character, and faithfulness? Explain.

Day Three: The word *meditate* is the pathway to your deepest knowledge of God. You meditate on all that you value. Based upon your thoughts today, what do you value?

Day Four: Explain what you think Madeleine L'Engle means when she says, "When there is no time for being there is no time for listening." How are you protecting your "being" time with the Lord?

Day Five: In your daily routine, what changes need to be made in order to produce the fruit of meditation in your life?

Character, the Strength of Wisdom

For the LORD gives wisdom, and from his mouth come knowledge and understanding.

Proverbs 2:6

Have you sought wisdom as instructed in the early Psalms? Believing James 1:5, perhaps you asked for abundant wisdom; after all, God promised to give liberally, holding nothing back. But soon after you prayed for wisdom, trouble arrived. Did you assume trouble was God's way of teaching you wisdom? Not always so. Wisdom is not learned through trouble, but God-given wisdom guides you through trouble.

Trouble isn't sent by God to teach wisdom, but as a consequence of living in the world, the inevitable trouble that comes can teach character. The apostle Paul wrote: "We also rejoice in our sufferings, because we know that suffering produces perseverance; perseverance, character" (Rom. 5:3–4). See, God's wisdom enables you to handle the trouble that builds the character you need.

The life of Solomon illustrates what happens when wisdom is not built upon the bedrock of strong character. As a young man he requested wisdom for governing God's people. God gave him wisdom and added to it riches, fame, and power. In fact, Solomon still holds the world record for wisdom among mere mortals. This is the man, however, whose flawed character in old age axed wisdom's mighty oak.

Don't be troubled, then, when your request for wisdom results in suffering. God is developing strength of character so you have both fortitude and foresight to walk in God's way, instead of failing like Solomon. Wisdom can guide you, but not hold you. When wisdom is supported by strong character, you'll be spared a downfall.

In Proverbs 4:6–8, Solomon encourages you to pay any price to gain wisdom: "Do not forsake wisdom, and she will protect you; love her, and she will watch over you. Wisdom is supreme; therefore get wisdom. Though it cost all you have, get understanding. Esteem her, and she will exalt you; embrace her, and she will honor you."

Do not fear the difficulties that develop the strength of character necessary to sustain wisdom. Fear the results of a weak character that collapses, spilling the rich fruit of wisdom everywhere. One such loss would be answered prayer. Proverbs 1:28 states,

"Then they will call to me but I will not answer; they will look for me but will not find me." Do you think Solomon experienced this at the end of his life?

Over the centuries, millions have gained from Solomon's wise sayings. Yet, his own epitaph read, "Here lies a wise man turned fool!" May yours read, "Here lies one whose strong character wore the crown of wisdom well."

■ Commune with God ■

Father, I seek you for wisdom and for the strength of character to wear the crown of wisdom well. In turn, help me exercise the wisdom to handle trouble, and in the throes of trouble remind me that true wisdom means turning to you and seeking your will and ways.

■ MAKE THE TEXT YOUR OWN ■

Day One: What key thought do you wish to remember from this meditation?

Day Two: Wisdom can guide you, but not hold you. Character does that. In what ways do you identify with this statement?

Day Three: What difference does it make in your life when you let wisdom guide you through trouble, rather than your own common sense? What sources do you turn to for wisdom?

Day Four: According to Solomon in Ecclesiastes 12:13b, what's the wisest thing a person can do? How can you apply this to your life?

Day Five: Dr. Warren Wiersbe says in his book *Be Mature,* "We need wisdom so we will not waste the opportunities God is giving us to mature." In what life experience have you learned the most? What did you learn?

The Right Time for Fire to Fall

O LORD, answer me, so these people will know
that you . . . are turning their hearts back again.

1 Kings 18:37

As a person of wisdom, you can see spiritual need a long way off. You can discern when others may be lacking spiritual development, or even perhaps living in sin. You know when someone needs a radical encounter with God, an encounter that shakes a person out of a spiritual stupor—a wake-up call from on high.

So, you pray for that person, but nothing happens. Soon you feel as though you're in a tug-of-war with God. The person of your concern continues in spiritual dullness, perhaps even rebellion. What's the problem?

It's not yet time for the fire to fall.

Take, for example, the dramatic story of Elijah facing the prophets of Baal (1 Kings 18:16–40), a playwright's dream come true. Here's how the story is formed.

- **Complication:** Elijah challenges the prophets of Baal to a "duel of the gods," in a contest between his God and theirs.
- **Staging:** The scene is set on a mountaintop with an awesome view of the open sky above and the sprawling Valley of Jezreel below.
- **Ultimatum:** The prophet challenges the nation to stop halting between two opinions (protagonist confronts antagonists), and decide between Jehovah and Baal based upon the outcome of the contest.
- **Villains:** The antagonists outnumber the hero four hundred and fifty to one.
- **Plot Thickens:** The people historically have followed Baal, but Elijah is about to shake their belief system and their entire sense of security by proving their god false.
- **Drama:** The prophets of Baal cut themselves to get their god to answer.
- **Suspense:** After taunting the false prophets and their god, Elijah deepens the difficulty for Jehovah by soaking his altar with water.

- **Resolution:** Elijah calls out to his God, fire drops from the sky, consumes the altar, the water, the rocks. The people turn back to Jehovah, immediately. Baal's prophets are slain.

The pace of this true story renders you breathless. You leave the theater atop Mount Carmel to descend into the valley of your concern. You're resolved to be an Elijah. You plead for dramatic fire, but see only dainty lightning bugs. You're almost ready to quit, wondering, *Why pray?*

Don't stop. God still drops fire in response to prayer, but only at the right time. It took three years of drought for Elijah's Israel to respond to falling fire.

So it is today. If divine fire falls before anyone cares, it's belittled as a coincidental shooting star, a natural disaster. But, when it falls at the right time, it produces repentance, even transformation. Look at Elijah's prayer more closely: "O LORD . . . let it be known today that you are God in Israel and that I am your servant and have done all these things at your command. Answer me . . . so these people will know that you, O LORD, are God, and that you are turning their hearts back again" (1 Kings 18:36–37).

God knows how long the drought needs to last in order to prepare hearts for the fire that proves the point. Faithfully pray through the long drought, as did Elijah, until that one moment in time when fire falls and all is changed.

▪ COMMUNE WITH GOD ▪

Father, help me to endure the wait so that I may behold the wonder. May the fire of your Spirit rise up in me as I wait for your fire to fall.

■ MAKE THE TEXT YOUR OWN ■

Day One: What key thought do you wish to remember from this
meditation?

Day Two: You know when someone needs a radical encounter
with God to shake him out of a spiritual stupor. For whom have
you prayed in such a way, and why? Is there someone you should
start praying for in this way?

Day Three: What might you do today to show God's love and concern to the person for whom you're praying?

Day Four: If divine fire falls before anyone really cares, it's belittled as a coincidental shooting star, a natural disaster. But, when
it falls at the right time, it produces repentance, even transformation. What can you do during the time of preparation for God's
divine appointments?

Day Five: In what dramatic ways have you seen, in response to
prayer, fire fall at the right time?

Mary: Blessed of God

Blessed is she who has believed that what the
Lord has said to her will be accomplished!

Luke 1:45

You never know when your prayers are about to collide with one of God's cosmic plans. Take the mother of Jesus, for instance.

Come with me to the village well in Nazareth. It's just an ordinary day. Look, there she is, Mary. Her feet glide softly, leaving little imprint on the path leading down to the well. She's beautiful in a pure sense, for she has gained favor with God—that's beyond genetic bestowment.

How so? Is she sinless? Impossible. Her parents are direct descendants of Adam, so she, too, was born with a sin nature. Grace, then, is the only answer. God has favored her through grace as he does all sinners who seek his salvation. To see Mary as sinless is to deny the depth of God's grace. God's Son would be born of the Holy Spirit through a sinner in order to redeem sinners (even the sinner who bore him). That need not be hard to accept, since God births his Son in sinners' hearts to this very day.

Mary is to be credited in the way she honors God's grace. As a virgin she holds the flower of her youth in sacred reserve for the man of God's choosing. She has devoted her heart to Jehovah God while living in the nondescript village of Nazareth, a village mocked as too common to produce anything good. Perhaps that's partly why God chose to bring the Messiah out of Nazareth. It represents the world's lowest common denominator.

Mary wants to please God, but expects nothing special from him. She simply anticipates spending her life cooking, drawing water, and raising the children of a carpenter who, in turn, cherishes her. That's all.

Suddenly Gabriel appears. Fragile Mary trembles. Gabriel! The mighty angel who only appears for extraordinary events.

"Greetings," the angel says. "You who are highly favored! The Lord is with you."

Is he crazy? Mary wonders.

"Do not be afraid," Gabriel continues. "You have found favor with God. You will be with child and give birth to a son, and you are to give him the name Jesus. He will be great and will be called the Son of the Most High. The Lord God will give him the throne

of his father David, and he will reign over the house of Jacob forever; his kingdom will never end."

"How will this be," Mary asks the angel, "since I am a virgin?"

"The Holy Spirit will come upon you, and the power of the
Most High will overshadow you. So the holy one to be born will
be called the Son of God" (Luke 1:28–35).

The angel leaves as suddenly as he came. Mary's alone, with
only her reflections. She hoists the jar of water to her head and
starts the mundane walk back home. But her life is eternally
changed by a word from God—a word she believes! Elizabeth
calls Mary blessed for this faith. The Bible calls her righteous for
it (Rom. 1:17).

There will be a lapse between the Word of God given and the
work of God done, thus raising a question in people's minds: By
whom is Mary pregnant? But faith doesn't worry about that. It
just believes God until his Word and his works are one!

Just as God offered Mary the chance to bring his greatest gift
into the world, he comes to you offering you the opportunity of
birthing gifts, through prayer, into the world. Mary said "yes."
Will you?

■ COMMUNE WITH GOD ■

Father, you offer to birth gifts into the world through me
just as you did Mary. I know that she birthed your Son.
What will you birth in me? Whatever your will, find in me
Mary's response when she said, "I am the Lord's servant.
May it be to me as you have said."

■ MAKE THE TEXT YOUR OWN ■

Day One: What key thought do you wish to remember from this meditation?

Day Two: Mary, mother of Jesus, wants to please God, but expects nothing special from him. Are you content with God alone? How do you show God that you love him for who he is, not merely for what he gives or does for you?

Day Three: Just as God offered Mary the chance to bring his greatest gift into the world, he comes to you offering you the opportunity of birthing gifts into the world. What gifts do you believe God has birthed, or is birthing, in and through your life?

Day Four: Notice how ready and available Mary was to receive God's Word. What can you do to keep your heart tender and obedient to the Word of God?

Day Five: Some rejected Mary and others questioned her character even though she was in the very center of God's will. In what ways have you faced rejection in doing what was right?

Nearer Than the Night

Why, O LORD, do you stand far off? Why do you
hide yourself in times of trouble?

Psalm 10:1

Alexander Solzhenitsyn wrote in his famous apostrophe to the Gulag, "Bless you, prison . . . for it was in you that I discovered that the meaning of earthly existence lies not as we have grown used to thinking, in prospering, but in the development of the soul."

Some of David's psalms seem melodramatic, peppered with groans and tears. But those are scenes of nocturnal wrestling on the deepest levels of the soul, scenes where the psalmist discovers what Solzhenitsyn found thousands of years later.

Perhaps right now you are living in such a psalm, trying to reassure yourself of sanity. No worthy person bypasses these haunts of darkness. You feel the chill of danger right to the core of your bones. Yet perspiration breaks out from a strange fever that mixes with the coldness of the night. You're engulfed in what the saints of old called "the dark night of the soul."

When you're in the midst of a crisis, God seems infinitely far removed, as though he has left the universe and shut the door behind him. You prayerfully recount his power to devastate armies, collapse walls, drop giants, and send fire. You know that with the lift of a finger he could sweep the crisis away; but still he does nothing.

Or so it seems. Actually, God is nearer than the night, literally dwelling inside of you, experiencing your anguish. God has chosen not to ride on high-flung clouds of ease while you languish in despair, a victim of fate. God chooses to enter in with you, experiencing all you face, firsthand, and even more.

It was God who first sent his Son to be tempted in all points such as you. This makes him a tender High Priest, interceding for you with understanding that exceeds your own. There's no experience in life that he has not experienced in greater measure. So you have God the Holy Spirit dwelling within, God the Son interceding above, and God the Father surrounding you with heartfelt sympathy.

God will work your deliverance: "Though he brings grief, he will show compassion, so great is his unfailing love. For he does not willingly bring affliction or grief to the children of men" (Lam. 3:32–33).

Why has God chosen to allow affliction, then enter into it with you? Why doesn't he just show himself mighty to deliver the moment you call? He could easily rise from his throne, speak one word, and dispel the night. But, no, there's something more important to God than showing his power to release pain, and that's his persistence to endure it with you. This is how he shapes you for those things that can't be had without it.

When blinded by misery, Job said, "I cry out to you, O God, but you do not answer" (30:20). Little did he know that a flood of blessing beyond his wildest dreams was about to be released from the hand of God. Job's life was to be on display as an encouragement to millions throughout the ages.

With irresistible eloquence, 2 Peter 1:19 calls us to faithful endurance: "And we have the word of the prophets made more certain, and you will do well to pay attention to it, as to a light shining in a dark place, until the day dawns and the morning star rises in your hearts."

Although the barren night feels tightly wrapped around you, pray until dawn when God breaks through!

▪ COMMUNE WITH GOD ▪

Father, I would prefer to write a soft, easy script for my life. But I know a hard one is a consequence of this world. Help me to gladly exchange softness for soundness. Thank you for being in the midst of the drama with me, not just as director, but as my empowerment.

■ MAKE THE TEXT YOUR OWN ■

Day One: What key thought do you wish to remember from this meditation?

Day Two: What event in your life reminds you of "the dark night of the soul"? What did you learn from it?

Day Three: As you reflect upon the dark times of your past, what do you believe God was accomplishing in your life? In what ways can you thank him for that time?

Day Four: What truths do you wish to remember when other dark times come?

Day Five: How can you encourage others going through dark times? What might you say or do? (You may wish to share this week's meditation with them.)

Hezekiah's Blunder

Remember, O LORD, how I have walked before you faithfully and with wholehearted devotion and have done what is good in your eyes.

Isaiah 38:3

It's tempting to follow the model of Hezekiah's prayer, but the results are fateful.

The prophet Isaiah had announced the king's soon-coming death. Not being advanced in years, Hezekiah couldn't bear the thought of dying. Therefore he turned his face to the wall, wept bitterly, and pleaded for a longer life. He appealed on the basis of his many years of goodness.

What a blunder! How did Hezekiah miss the truth about the evil in the human heart? Had he missed too many Sabbaths in the synagogue? Did he fail so-called Genesis 101? But one doesn't need to be a New Testament scholar either to understand human depravity. After all, Paul's revelation of the hopeless condition of the human heart in Romans 3 is lifted line upon line from the Old Testament.

No, Hezekiah was without excuse for appealing to God based upon his personal goodness. Yet similar arguments are presented to God by many today, perhaps even by you. Do you think God should bless you because you have been good? Do you view God as unfair when something painful enters your life? Hezekiah considered his good works as meritorious rather than reasonable service. You demean God as being less intelligent than yourself when you question the way he handles a situation.

What's the result of such arrogance? In Hezekiah's case, God granted his request. What a wild turn of events, however, when Hezekiah gained the desired answer, but not the desired results! Hezekiah did receive fifteen extra years of life. His crisis passed, but, strangely, so did his dependence upon God.

Pride resurrected its ugly head. When foreign kings came to see the man delivered by God from certain death, Hezekiah showcased his gold, not his God. Hezekiah then paraded the pagans through his assortment of military paraphernalia—something he would never have dreamed of doing during his obedient years.

While Hezekiah's behavior is difficult to understand, it teaches several lessons. The obvious one is that miracles can't guard the heart from blunders. Only obedience in faith does that. But two more lessons quickly rise for observation. First, never appeal to

God on the basis of your goodness. Appeal only on the basis of God's grace and the honor of his name.

Second, commit yourself to persistent prayer for the ability to properly handle the answered prayer for his purpose and glory. The God you need to bring an answer is the same God needed to sustain you in the answer so that you won't repeat Hezekiah's blunder.

■ COMMUNE WITH GOD ■

Father, I ask you to grant me a proper view of myself, of my ever-present readiness to violate you and even go back on my word. Keep me mindful to look to you alone, both for the answers you choose and my ability to handle them in faithfulness.

■ MAKE THE TEXT YOUR OWN ■

Day One: What key thought do you wish to remember from this meditation?

Day Two: Upon what basis do you appeal to God before his throne?

Day Three: How do you perceive the ministry God has given you—meritorious or reasonable service? Explain.

Day Four: If you received your heart's desire today, what negative or positive effect do you believe it would have upon your character?

Day Five: Ask the Lord to help you understand and accept the truths of Romans 3. Ask him to help you more fully understand that it's through mercy and grace that he hears and answers your prayers.

But If Not

He will rescue us from your hand, O king. But even if he does not, we want you to know, O king, that we will not serve your gods.

Daniel 3:17–18

*F*aith empowers prayer, but what is faith? Is it merely a mustered-up feeling that forces God to act as you desire? Or is it the release of all rights to God, trusting him to answer according to his wisdom?

The latter was the view of the three Hebrew children Shadrach, Meshach, and Abednego. The story is well known, how they wouldn't bow to the image of gold established by the king of Babylon. The furnace of punishment was heated seven times greater than necessary to burn them alive. In fact, the king's men perished while adding fuel to the fire.

In human terms, this would have been a good time for the three Hebrew men to negotiate or even compromise. They could have bent their knee to the image, but not their hearts. Or they could have pacified this momentary whim of the king in order to stay alive and be future witnesses for Jehovah.

Nebuchadnezzar was white hot with rage to think of their insolence. He had favored them, lifting them from hard labor to serve in the palace. Still, they ignored his edict. *Impudent ingrates,* he must have thought. The fire in the furnace paled compared to his rage.

It's in this context that these young men made one of the greatest statements, a classic of all time: "If we are thrown into the blazing furnace, the God we serve is able to save us from it, and he will rescue us from your hand, O King. But even if he does not . . . we will not serve your gods or worship the image of gold you have set up" (Dan. 3:17–18).

Now that's faith! It took absolute trust in God to do what was right whether it meant deliverance or demise. Job said it this way: "Though he slay me, yet will I hope in him" (Job 13:15).

This kind of faith made three Hebrew men unstoppable. They wouldn't negotiate with unbelief. Their uncompromising faith forced pagans to face God head-on. There was no way around it. Their willingness to die for God compelled the world to consider Jehovah.

This faith also gave Jehovah options in how to reveal himself. In this case it was through deliverance. What was the result? This may have been the very event that jolted Nebuchadnezzar toward his eventual conversion. Beyond this it took seven years of insanity to prepare the pagan's heart, but he did eventually honor Jehovah: "Therefore I decree that the people of any nation or language who say anything against the God of Shadrach, Meshach and Abednego be cut into pieces and their houses be turned into piles of rubble, for no other god can save in this way" (Dan. 3:29).

Likewise, use every opportunity in your life to let God prove himself as he desires. Rather than consider the impact of consequences upon your personal situation, consider only how your faith may best honor God. Praying in faith that God will work wisely in your situation, stand firm on the ultimate expression of faith: *But if not . . . !*

■ COMMUNE WITH GOD ■

Surely, Father, it was not an easy choice for the three Hebrew youths to honor you with such faith. Help me to mature to their level of faith and be able to so trust you amid threatening circumstances that I can say, "But if not, I still will not betray my God."

■ MAKE THE TEXT YOUR OWN ■

Day One: What key thought do you wish to remember from this meditation?

Day Two: According to Hebrews 11:1, what is faith? What biblical illustration helps you explain your definition of faith?

Day Three: What other examples in the Bible come to mind of those who acted upon God's faithfulness, character, and Word? What examples come to mind of Christ rebuking those who did not trust him?

Day Four: Read the "faith chapter" in Hebrews 11, then fill in the blank:

By faith _____ believed God for _____ ,
            (your name)   (act of God)

even though the present circumstances seem to prove otherwise.

Day Five: It's true that God loves you unconditionally and there's nothing you can do to make him love you more or love you any less. However, based upon a lack of faith or trust, you can displease him (see Heb. 11:6). Think of specific examples when loved ones didn't trust you or believe what you told them. How did you feel? How do you think God feels when you don't trust him?

Fasting for Sovereign Solutions

So I turned to the Lord God and pleaded with him in prayer and petition, in fasting, and in sackcloth and ashes.

Daniel 9:3

The people of the Bible didn't fast in order to overcome a reluctance in God—as though fasting would twist God's arm to do something. Rather, they fasted in order to see God do the things he promised. Look at the many examples of this in the Scriptures:

- **Moses** knew God willed the release of Israel from Egypt and would lead her to the Promised Land; after all, it was God who revealed his intention at the burning bush (Exod. 3:2). Yet, when God threatened to destroy Israel and start a new nation under Moses, the man of God spent forty days and nights fasting for Israel to be spared.

- **Daniel** prayed for Israel's deliverance from Babylon, not to force God, but to establish on earth what God told Jeremiah he would do (Dan. 9:2). Daniel felt God's will had to be prayed into reality on earth, otherwise he would have read Jeremiah's account, then flitted his time away in fanciful folly. Instead, he fasted in sackcloth and ashes.

- **Paul**, too, had God's will clearly revealed. He was not only called to be an apostle in dramatic fashion, he was told he would be a witness of the truth by suffering much persecution. Although Paul had access to Jesus' strong words, "I will build my church" (Matt. 16:18), he often engaged in fasting to see it come to pass.

Why does God require such self-sacrifice? Perhaps that question can't be completely answered. Of this you can be certain, however: Self-sacrifice is central to God's nature. It's the quintessence of love and will be the disposition of the coming kingdom of God.

Since divine law and justice require that all sin be atoned for with blood, your salvation was secured through the self-sacrifice of God's own Son. God couldn't simply wave his hand and pardon you without an act of self-sacrifice on the cross. Likewise the grand movements of God, whether impacting global trends or personal family needs, require self-sacrifice.

What you can also know is that the deeper the self-sacrifice, the greater the divine entrustment, and the greater the exaltation (1 Peter 5:6). For instance, Jesus' sacrificial obedience unto death won him a name above all other names. Submitting to injustice gained for him the highest position of authority over all of creation.

Central to fasting, then, seems to be self-sacrifice, temporarily cutting yourself off from your life-support, somewhat as Christ cut himself off from heaven's support. As Christ sacrificed his life to draw you into God's will for salvation, so you must sacrifice some comfort to establish God's will in heaven on earth.

There's no merit to be found in fasting, just reasonable service. It's not a matter of applying pressure to God. It's an intentional sacrifice to see God do what he already promised.

▪ COMMUNE WITH GOD ▪

Father, find me willing and honored to sacrifice for you. My God and Savior, make me more like you—willing to give completely, to lose wholeheartedly my wants for your will.

■ MAKE THE TEXT YOUR OWN ■

Day One: What key thought do you wish to remember from this meditation?

Day Two: What sacrifices are you making to see God move in your current situation?

Day Three: What do you want God to do that he's already promised to do?

Day Four: In his book *God's Chosen Fast* Arthur Wallis says, "Some things just won't budge without fasting." For what purpose, or for whom, do you believe God may be calling you to fast?

Day Five: Fasting is serious business. In preparing for a fast ask the Lord to show you what kind of fast you should enter (partial or total), for how long, and for what purpose. Also read *God's Chosen Fast* by Arthur Wallis and obtain your doctor's permission.

Delight and Desire

Delight yourself in the Lord and he will give you the desires of your heart.

Psalm 37:4

Desire is a wonderful part of your existence, a distinguishing mark that sets you apart from all else created in the six days of Genesis. Lower creatures may understand instincts to kill for food, care for their young, or purr for petting, but never can animals desire and form an intelligent plan.

You, however, are flooded with desire—a force backed by thought, memory, and foresight. This is intelligence, which allows you to perceive, reason, and change your mind. Desire is an urge to gain what you don't have, and it's a most extraordinary capacity since it gives you a limited sense of creativity, something of the image of God in you. In other words, you can desire to bring into existence something that's not there.

God doesn't oppose desire. On the contrary, he created it. But, when desire is driven by self, it becomes destructive. Sin, which is unleashed selfishness, throws desire out of control. Desire, then, is a God-given force that can either direct or destroy your life. Therefore, it's critical that desire be brought into its proper use when you come to pray, otherwise great frustration and confusion will result when God seems to ignore your prayers.

Properly directed desire is found in Psalm 37:4: "Delight yourself in the LORD and he will give you the desires of your heart." Your problem begins when you reverse that verse. You instinctively seek to get God to first fulfill the desires of your heart, with a promise that you'll then delight yourself in him. You may promise, for instance, that if God will bless you financially, you'll give him a certain amount. Isn't that an insult to the Lord who owns the gold in every mine? Or you may promise that if God resolves a major crisis, you'll be more faithful in some religious practice. Isn't that ridiculous in light of the fact that complete devotion to God is the very purpose of your existence in the first place? Endless are the deals offered to God, always placing the fulfillment of desire ahead of delight in God.

God simply said desire will be fulfilled when you reverse that order. Delight yourself in God, then he'll fulfill the desires of your heart.

"But," you argue, "if I'm delighted with the Lord, then my desires will be his desires and not my own." Right! You've got it. But before that makes you feel caught like a bear in a trap, remember that apart from him, your desires are untrustworthy. It's a fateful blunder to assume that whatever you intensely desire must be alright. The psalmist knew better and prayed in Psalm 119:36, "Turn my heart toward your statutes and not toward selfish gain." He had learned not to trust the natural wisdom of his heart.

In both the Psalms and Proverbs you're exhorted to gain divine wisdom, the guiding light of desire, at all cost. Proverbs 2:6 states, "For the LORD gives wisdom, and from his mouth come knowledge and understanding."

Once again it boils down to the contest for supremacy: Are God's desires supreme, or are yours? Who is most wise? David made the choice and prayed in Psalm 139:23–24, "Search me, O God, and know my heart; test me and know my anxious thoughts. See if there is any offensive way in me."

As you pray, remember: When you prevent personal desire from blocking sovereign designs, God can do his greatest work.

▪ COMMUNE WITH GOD ▪

Father, desire is a strong force, but it is simply another area for me to submit to you. May I so love you that your desires and mine become one. Turn my desire to your delight, so that your delight will be my desire.

■ MAKE THE TEXT YOUR OWN ■

Day One: What key thought do you wish to remember from this meditation?

Day Two: What are the strongest desires of your heart?

Day Three: What do you want God to do for you or through you? Why?

Day Four: In what ways are you evidencing God working out your desires?

Day Five: Sometimes our desires can consume us and our priorities get out of order. What areas of your life may need reprioritizing in order to focus on Christ rather than the desires of your heart?

Acknowledging God in Relationship

Then you will know that I am the LORD your
God, who brought you out from under the
yoke.

Exodus 6:7

*S*uppose a baby is born with little chance to live. Medical science is stretched to the limit as the family prays. The baby lives and grows up to become an Olympic champion. One person will call this an amazing coincidence, while another labels it an act of God. What's the difference? One person acknowledges fate, while another acknowledges God as the ruler of life.

To acknowledge God for the full depth of who he is demands more than a nod of the head. It requires a bending of the knees. You're worshiping the one who's infinitely above all that he made, yet who enters your deepest hurt on the lowest level. There's nothing God won't do to get you properly related to himself, since your eternal well-being depends upon it. So God uses both deliverance and destruction as a means of revelation.

God delivered Israel out of Egypt and crushed opposing nations, so they would acknowledge the true God. Throughout the Old Testament the divine purpose, then, in both deliverance and judgment, was that the people would know he is God.

Simply look up the word *know* in your concordance. See what people through time have seen? God isn't a bully avenging hurt feelings over your rebellion. Your rebellion simply demands that God use radical means to teach you who he is!

Why do you have such a hard time acknowledging God? Probably because doing so is also an acknowledgment of what you're not. He alone is God, not you. He alone is all-sufficient, you're not. This rubs against the grain of the lie inbred in you from Adam's fall: "You will be like God" (Gen. 3:5).

Archimedes, the Greek inventor, declared, "Give me a place to stand and I will move the world." Strangely, upon death, it wasn't the world, but just a little lowly soil that swallowed him.

Believing a lie, you try to be your own god, acting as though you can live your own life your own way without consequences. You start by reshaping God into an image of your liking, thereby elevating yourself while lowering him. In response God lovingly teaches you the most important lesson of life: your need for desperate dependence upon him—not just for one item, but for breath, heartbeat, and existence itself! Sometimes this is done by deliverance, other times by destruction. It's your pride, however, that often makes this a painful process.

In all these lessons God simply brings you back to reality, the reality of who he is. Only when you acknowledge this are you fit for a relationship with him. It can be said of all relationships that the deeper the interdependence, the greater the relationship. Conversely, the deeper the independence, the less the relationship. First, acknowledge him as he revealed himself, without rewriting the script. Second, acknowledge your absolute dependence upon him for every part of life. Then his ears are open and his heart attentive to your prayers.

■ COMMUNE WITH GOD ■

Holy, holy, holy, Lord God Almighty. I worship you in all your majesty and splendor. I honor you, adore you, and acknowledge you. Help me to shamelessly carry praise of you before all men at all times.

■ Make the Text Your Own ■

Day One: What key thought do you wish to remember from this meditation?

Day Two: On a piece of paper, make two columns, one headed "Experience" and the other "Revelation." Now write out in what experiences God has revealed himself to you in a profound way. What did he reveal to you about himself through these experiences?

Day Three: When you reshape God into an image of your liking, you elevate yourself while lowering him. Reflect upon the times when you brought God down to your level of thinking—times perhaps when you condemned yourself. Were they times of failure, success, deep loss, or mediocrity?

Day Four: At a certain age, a child no longer wishes to take the hand of his parent to cross the street, desiring to claim his independence. In what area of life would you rather go it alone than take your Father's hand?

Day Five: It can be said of all relationships that the deeper the interdependence, the greater the relationship. Conversely, the greater the independence, the less the relationship. Explain how this statement relates to you and those closest to you.

Acknowledging God in Prayer

But I the Lord will answer them . . . so that
people may see and know, may consider and
understand, that the hand of the Lord has done
this, that the Holy One of Israel has created it.

Isaiah 41:17, 20

*I*t's understandable when pets show limited appreciation for all that you do for them. While cats purr and dogs wag their tails, you don't expect them to hold a conversation explaining the depth of their gratitude.

But you and I are not pets who belong to God. Having made humans the highest of all creation, God has every right to expect more. He empowered you to remember the past, reason the present, and dream the future. You and I can even conceive of the unseen: gravity, air, time. Further, God gave us an extraordinary capacity for thoughts, emotions, and aesthetics, plus motivation that goes far beyond mere existence: "He has also set eternity in the hearts of men" (Eccles. 3:11).

But people with little or no interest in prayer are as nose-to-the-grass oriented as a creature. They live out the innate belief that they're the essence of existence, that their interest is all that matters, that they're somehow self-sustaining. And when God allows trouble to bring them back to reality, they squall as though God is a cruel ogre messing up their plans.

A prayerless person, then, lives in the illusion of an arrogance that believes the lie: "You will be as God." This is the ultimate non-reality. Conversely, people of prayer have overcome the garden fantasy presented by Satan. Through conversion they've come to reality: "You are not God."

Acknowledging God by being a person of prayer, therefore, isn't entering a world of spiritual make-believe; it's reentry into reality. It is tragic when God must go to extremes to bring you there. For God to bring Israel to reality demanded captivity, drought, disease, and death. Still, she has not fully returned.

In the United States, laws are firmly in place forbidding that God be acknowledged on school property on school time—that is, until there's a crisis, such as the Columbine massacre. Then students and faculty alike call out to God both on school property and on school time. The news media join in the call for prayer. When the chaos dies down, there's a return to man-made laws that ban the creator of all law—until the next crisis, that is.

What about you? Do you acknowledge God by choice, or must it come by chastening? The depth to which you acknowledge God in prayer reveals the depth to which you have come to reality.

So be found faithful, acknowledging and exalting God at all times, in all circumstances, so that your prayers may always be heard.

■ Commune with God ■

Father, continue to extend your mercy and grace to people, like me, who neglect to acknowledge you. But find me faithful, that my prayers may be heard. Give me the strength and help me find the discipline to be deliberate in my commitment to you.

■ Make the Text Your Own ■

Day One: What key thought do you wish to remember from this meditation?

Day Two: In what ways do your prayers depict that God rules and reigns in your life?

Day Three: "A prayerless person, then, lives in the illusion of an arrogance that believes the lie: 'You will be like God.'" What do you think is meant by this statement?

Day Four: "Acknowledging God by being a person of prayer isn't entering a world of spiritual make-believe, it's reentry into reality." What do you think is meant by this statement?

Day Five: When most pressed by his gigantic toil, Martin Luther said, "I have so much to do, that I can't get on without three hours a day of praying." How do you relate to this?

Weep for Just a Little While

You will grieve, but your grief will turn to joy.

John 16:20

Weeping didn't end at the resurrection. The Man of Sorrows still weeps, as do those who walk with him. When God's tender heart collides with the harsh arrogance of sinful man, tears flow from both the Savior and his servants. That's how divine work gets done.

Take courage, however. Weeping is only for a season. Jesus said, "Are you asking one another what I meant when I said, 'In a little while you will see me no more, and then after a little while you will see me'? I tell you the truth, you will weep and mourn while the world rejoices. You will grieve, but your grief will turn to joy" (John 16:19–20).

It's during the span of time between Christ's departure and return that the Man of Sorrows tearfully walks with his disciples, experiencing both the agony and ecstasy of building his kingdom. Herein lies a tension. Having seen the suffering Savior's death, your soul is liberated. Having heard the mighty Messiah's words, you long for his righteous reign. Like John on the Isle of Patmos, you transcend your prison, see and hear eternal things, then, for a short season, return to your dank prison cell—a cell invaded by the stench of godlessness.

Tears flow from grandparents who care for the children of their drug-addicted sons and daughters. Tears flow over children whose hearts are swept away in the tide of sensuality, children whose eyes once danced with sweet, innocent laughter. Tears flow over the inequity and injustice compounded by those who call evil good, and good evil, who drag sin along by cords of deceit (Isa. 5:18–20).

Tears may flow, but you are still a prisoner of hope (Zech. 9:12). You mourn over what is because you long for what is to be. With a clear view of how things must be, you're torn by what is. Strange, isn't it, that mourning and joy become bedfellows, at least for a little while. Joy abounds as you ascend the mountain where you're taught to walk in God's paths (Isa. 2:3). Joy results from the life of the Spirit and the wholeness of obedience. Then back to your home, your street, your world, where you return to mourn with the Man of Sorrows until he comes to reign.

Sharing tears with the Man of Sorrows is not just enduring grief or awaiting your turn for joy. Your cries to God result in mighty, divine acts of redemption: a son or daughter is delivered to new life, a hopeless marriage is saved, moral weakness turns into steel-like integrity, unbelief melts into faith. And these divine triumphs—one here, one there—are preparing the people who will reign with Christ in the coming new world.

The psalmist saw tears as an investment of labor resulting in an abundant harvest. He wrote, "Those who sow in tears will reap with songs of joy" (Ps. 126:5).

Mike Mason, the brilliant author of *The Gospel According to Job,* wrote regarding Job's sorrows, "It is Job's ultimate knowledge of his own utter helplessness that becomes the very ground upon which he stands as he reaches out boldly to shake the throne of God."

It's in suffering that you learn to pray. It's in suffering that you're conformed to Christ. It's in suffering that your eternal station is established. Paul Billheimer wrote in *Don't Waste Your Sorrows:* "There is no love without self-giving. There is no self-giving without pain. Therefore, there is no love without suffering." Suffering, then, is not an intruding monster violating your tranquility, but a loving servant in the hand of the living God bent on your eternal well-being.

Press on! Soon the scene will change. The time will come, "When the kings of the earth who committed adultery with her and shared her luxury see the smoke of her burning, [and then] they will weep and mourn over her" (Rev. 18:9). The mourning of the world is a smoke that will never clear; your sorrow will. So you may weep, but just for a little while.

◾ COMMUNE WITH GOD ◾

Father, help me to remember that tears are a powerful form of prayer, cleansing the heart for the entrance of joy. Find me as Paul, wanting to share in the sufferings of Christ that I may share in the glory of his resurrection power.

■ MAKE THE TEXT YOUR OWN ■

Day One: What key thought do you wish to remember from this meditation?

Day Two: Like John on the Isle of Patmos, in what ways do you transcend your prison, see and hear eternal things, then, for a short season, return to your dank prison cell?

Day Three: What has sorrow, pain, or grief accomplished in your life?

Day Four: If pain and sorrow hadn't entered your life, what kind of person do you think you'd be today?

Day Five: In what ways have you seen your character transformed into the image of Christ through suffering?

Nap with Jesus

The disciples went and woke him, saying,
"Lord, save us!"

Matthew 8:25

The stories of the Bible could pose a nightmare for people who like neatly packaged endings. The Bible is too brilliant for that. Stories such as Jesus and the disciples on the storm-tossed sea are open-ended, giving way to varied applications. Picture these stories as ships of truth with a thousand lifelines tossed into the sea so that people can grab them and be pulled to safety from any direction.

Such is the case when Jesus rebuked his disciples for awakening him in a state of panic amid the howling winds and threatening swells. Why did he rebuke their less-than-mustard-seed faith? The answer can be found in a multitude of applications, each offering a lifeline for someone to get on board and learn of faith.

It could be that he rebuked them for not having the faith to speak to the winds and quiet the storm as he did. That's one possibility. But let me suggest another. Is it possible that Jesus was rebuking them for being up on the deck holding forth in a panic-stricken watch instead of napping with him below?

Consider this idea as it applies to prayer. There's a place for steadfast prayer before God's throne. But there's a point when it becomes the nagging of unbelief—a sure sign that one hasn't learned to abide in Christ. What was the difference between Jesus and his disciples on that blustery, life-threatening night? Jesus obviously had an abiding relationship with the Father that was so rich, so deep, so settled that he could nap amid the storm. He knew his Father would allow nothing, no matter how intimidating, to stop the purpose of his Son's life. The disciples obviously hadn't reached that point in the development of their faith. So they undoubtedly grabbed Jesus' robes to shake him awake as they screamed, "Save us!"

Again, be assured that it's proper to bring an issue before the Lord many times, but be guarded against vain babbling. Watch out for persistent prayer that's actually driven by a lack of confidence in God.

If you don't know someone very well, then persistence may be necessary. For instance, you may have to bang down the door of an insurance agency with repeated requests to settle a claim. But if you're making a request of a father whom you know well, and he makes a promise, you can ask once, then take a nap. You know the answer will come. That's the difference between those who can nap as a storm rages around them and others who thrash about, wrestling the storm within their very souls.

Jesus knew that he didn't need to explain, demand, persist, repeat, then throw a fit when his journey was interrupted by a storm. He probably started his day with his usual "Thy will be done" prayer and knew that it would be done! He surely read the psalms many times, believing the irreversible faithfulness of his Father's character. So he napped.

The evidence, then, that you've reached such a state of abiding, knowing, trusting, and resting in God is that storm time can be naptime. This doesn't ignore the raging reality on the sea. Rather it rests in a greater reality—the God who commands the sea.

So present your case to God, then take a nap, no matter how violent the storm.

▪ COMMUNE WITH GOD ▪

Father, I'm guilty of dishonoring you with panicked persistence that reveals how little I know you. Help me to remember that storms will come to everyone. May I know you well enough to determine when I'm to rebuke the storm and when I'm to take a nap—by faith!

■ MAKE THE TEXT YOUR OWN ■

Day One: What key thought do you wish to remember from this meditation?

Day Two: How would you describe an abiding relationship with the Father?

Day Three: In what particular areas of your prayer life may you be praying in vain repetition?

Day Four: What storm has taken place in your life when you felt God was napping and didn't seem concerned about your circumstances? Even though God never forsook you, why do you think he seemed so distant?

Day Five: What hymn or chorus would best convey your trust in God's faithfulness?

Fight Emotional Overload

That night they caught nothing.

John 21:3

Your emotions can only handle so much (good or bad) before you unplug. That's all there is to it.

You may find, for instance, that Christmas excesses like glitter, sugar, and gifts—as good as they are—dump you into January with a sense of relief and a need to recover. On the other hand, let too many things go wrong (the car needs repairs, the plumbing leaks, the kids fight, you lose your job) and you tend to blow up.

You're better structured to handle highs and lows that aren't so high and low. Mountains are thrilling to view but climbing them is altogether another thing, something a rare few accomplish. Most people can more easily manage gentle, rolling hills.

The Bible doesn't explain why Peter, following the severe emotional drain of Christ's crucifixion and then the exhilaration of two postresurrection appearances, said to his fellow disciples, "I'm going fishing." But the disciples readily responded, "We're going too" (John 21:3). It appears as though the whole bunch could cope no more. You've probably been at this point, and probably will be again.

This is the time when your prayer life can get derailed. You just can't deal with any more emotional highs or lows. At one time you feel as though you can nearly touch God's face. At other times, his face seems turned away. It's unnerving.

Your response? You say, "I'm goin' fishin'." You're going to do something else—something more predictable, offering quicker gratification, with less strain. And God doesn't stop you. So there you are on the sea, doing what you know best, what comes easily. (For the disciples it was fishing.)

But going fishing doesn't work, For you—just as for the disciples— there's not so much as a nibble all night! Now that's troublesome. You've added fatigue to your emotional overload; it's not good. It's now that you need some genuine help—the real kind, not just a card with a cute saying. The Lord knows that, so he shows up in person.

"Friend, haven't you any fish?" What a question. It's pretty obvious.

"No," you reply.

"Throw your net on the right side of the boat and you will find some," he says (John 21:5–6).

The haul is beyond your dreams. What is Jesus doing? He doesn't rebuke you for your excursion on the sea, your return to a lesser call. He understands overload. But he also shows you that nothing, including fishing, can succeed without him. He says, "Apart from me you can do nothing" (John 15:5).

The next step is breakfast—life returning to normalcy. Christian life isn't all crucifixion or resurrection. It's a quiet breakfast too. Your emotions calm. Your body readjusts. Your mind opens. Now you're ready for his words, "Follow me!" (John 21:19).

He called you to be a fisher of men. Emotional overload drove you to be a fisher of, well, let's say, just fish. Now it's back to the divine call. "You're to fish for men, but you can only do so by following me," he says.

So, you've had your little hiatus on the sea, now it's back to the throne, and time to pray.

■ COMMUNE WITH GOD ■

Thank you, Father, that you're patient during my times of overload. There are times when I try to work it out by escaping to the security of the past. Thank you for welcoming me back to your throne, as though I've never been away. Lord, I want to stay here with you.

■ MAKE THE TEXT YOUR OWN ■

Day One: What key thought do you wish to remember from this meditation?

Day Two: Fill in the blank: When I'm overloaded, overwhelmed with life's highs and lows, I find retreat in _____. Is this a good thing? Why or why not?

Day Three: How has God met you in your time of emotional over-load?

Day Four: What Scripture texts come to mind that bring peace?

Day Five: Sometimes it's important to get alone for a half-day, entire day, or maybe longer, for a spiritual retreat. How might you get away for an extended period of time? How might you be refreshed and restored as a fisher of men?

Lest You Fall

Watch and pray so that you will not fall into temptation.

Matthew 26:41

Jesus wasn't only concerned with his crucifixion that evening in the Garden of Gethsemane. He also knew the impact his death would have upon his disciples. That's why he commanded them to pray.

Instead, they slept. The consequences were dire. By dawn Peter violated his own commitment to Christ with a flat-out denial. By the evening of the crucifixion all the disciples hid—fearful and defeated.

Who knows what conversations were held after Christ's death. Surely, they were conversations laced with self-doubt, disappointment, and reassessment. The followers of Jesus, then, were no different than we are today: They were vulnerable. That's why in the garden Jesus told them to pray, lest they fall.

There's a temptation—different for each of us—that can bring us down. God knows what it is, and so does Satan, I'm sure. You probably don't know which one will buckle your faith should the pressure become great enough, driving you to violate all you stand for.

That happened to Peter. Only a few hours earlier, as the disciples ate the last supper, Jesus had predicted his death. Peter lifted high his sword of loyalty, declaring, "Even if all fall away, I will not" (Mark 14:29).

Perhaps the room echoed with a burst of, "Bravo . . . bravo," mingled with a smattering of applause and a hearty, "Amen!" Peter's bravura strutted. Incredulously, his courage gave him confidence to ignore Jesus' request to pray. So he slept. Or did he really understand what Jesus meant? Not many hours slipped by before even the darkness could not hide the ghastly words that came from his own mouth: "I don't know him!" Not just once did Peter say this, but three times. The words revealed the disfigurement of his soul.

Suddenly, the cock crowed, just as Jesus predicted. The shrill sound penetrated Peter's heart with guilt and shame. All that he believed about himself was shattered. His self-assurance lay before him, mortally wounded.

Peter fell. So will you, if you're not committed to prayer. So will I.

Jesus taught us to pray, "Lead us not into temptation, but deliver us from the evil one" (Matt. 6:13). It's proper to translate this, "Lead us not into hard testing, but deliver us from the evil one."

Temptation isn't always some delightful enticement. Sometimes it's hard testing. Sometimes it's being thrown like an egg against a rock. Only God can strengthen you while orchestrating your circumstances to keep you from breaking. Paul wrote, "No temptation has seized you except what is common to man. And God is faithful; he will not let you be tempted beyond what you can bear. But when you are tempted, he will also provide a way out so that you can stand up under it" (1 Cor. 10:13).

If this is true, then why do so many fall? Either they ignore God's way of escape, or they're sleeping instead of praying.

It was Peter who warned, "Be self-controlled and alert. Your enemy the devil prowls around like a roaring lion looking for someone to devour" (1 Peter 5:8). He should know. He had first-hand experience at both Gethsemane and Calvary.

Prayer, then, isn't a passive exercise for the weak, but the protective power-center of the strong. Rise up! It's time to vigilantly watch and pray!

■ COMMUNE WITH GOD ■

Father, my spirit is willing, but my flesh is weak. Often my will is weak too. Help me to prove steadfast, not in boasting about how strong and faithful I'll be, but through prayer, discovering how strong and faithful you make me.

■ MAKE THE TEXT YOUR OWN ■

Day One: What key thought do you wish to remember from this meditation?

Day Two: What steps are you taking to become self-controlled and alert?

Day Three: In what way(s) might you feel like a failure?

Day Four: If you had one thing to do over again in life, what would it be? Why? What would you do instead?

Day Five: Life can be full of "if only's" and "what if's." One of Satan's masterful schemes is to keep you inoperable as you dwell on such things. It's natural to have fears and regrets, but what you do with such thoughts is most important. Identify your worst fears and regrets. Now lay them at the cross, ask forgiveness where needed, claim God's loving grace to protect you from the evil one, and move forward for the cause of Jesus Christ.

Dress Matters

"Friend," he asked, "how did you get in here without wedding clothes?"

Matthew 22:12

Granted, this is a come-as-you-are era. Over the decades quite a war took place before those who dress down defeated those who dress up. There's a sad by-product as the smoke clears and finger-pointing stops; along with the down-home look has come the devaluation of events and ceremony.

There are times when dressing up is essential. In Matthew 22 Jesus doesn't make light of proper attire for a wedding. He questions how a down-dresser got into the event. In fact, the casual fellow is bound and kicked out. What's the point of the parable? Is Jesus making it a law that you must dress up for weddings? No. His point is that proper dress is required to come before God (or enter his kingdom). The parable closes with the famed words, "For many are invited, but few are chosen" (Matt. 22:14).

What's the basis for being chosen, then? Dress! Are you dressed for the marriage supper of the Lamb? Are you presentable for God's eyes? Are you dressed for the kingdom?

Forget tuxedos versus blue jeans, tie-dyed tee shirts versus French cuffs. That's not the issue at all. Heaven's required dress is the garment of righteousness. Is your heart clothed with the unrighteous nature of sin, or the righteous nature of Jesus Christ?

The garment of Christ's righteousness was bought for you by God (1 Peter 3:18), provided for you by God (Rom. 1:17; 3:22; 5:19), and placed on you by God (Isa. 61:10; Zech. 3:4–5).

You cannot say, "I can't afford it," since it was paid for by Christ. You cannot say, "Surely God won't put it on me," when that's the clear offer of the gospel. You cannot argue, "I can't be good enough for God," when God offers to dress you in his goodness.

You could never stand before God on your own merit. Never! Your righteousness, your best efforts at right living, are as filthy rags (Isa. 64:6). The only way you can ever come before God is by wearing the garment of Christ's righteousness.

Anyone not wearing the garment will be bound and thrown out of the kingdom. Anyone not wearing the garment cannot enter God's presence to pray (unless the cry is, "Be merciful to me, a sinner").

Once you don a garment you're expected to live up to the role designated. A five-star general's uniform is never put on a first-class private, but once a general's uniform is placed on a person, he's expected to be a general.

Having been dressed in the righteousness of Christ, you are commanded to live a life worthy of your calling (Eph. 4:1). Live righteously! John wrote, "Fine linen stands for the righteous acts of the saints" (Rev. 19:8). Clothing and conduct are one and the same.

You're to come before God wearing Christ's garment of righteousness (that gives you the right of entrance), with corresponding righteous acts (that's reasonable service), and pray. What's the result? "The prayer of a righteous man is powerful and effective" (James 5:16).

When properly attired in Christ, then, you get great things done by prayer because when you're standing before God, dress matters!

■ COMMUNE WITH GOD ■

Father, thank you for providing the garment of your Son's righteousness for all who believe. I confess where I've failed to dignify my garment with proper actions. Trusting your forgiveness, I commit myself anew to the acts that honor the robe. Hear my prayers, Lord, and have mercy.

■ MAKE THE TEXT YOUR OWN ■

Day One: What key thought do you wish to remember from this meditation?

Day Two: Describe the moment in time when you invited Christ to be the Lord of your life and Savior of your soul. If you haven't done so, why not bow your head right now and ask him into your heart (read John 3)?

Day Three: How would you feel if someone showed up at your wedding in inappropriate attire?

Day Four: According to this week's reference, what garments are you wearing when you enter God's throne room in prayer?

Day Five: What does Ephesians 4:1 mean to you? What steps are you taking to fulfill it?

Faithful until Dawn

Throw your net on the right side of the boat
and you will find some.

John 21:6

Often, praying is like the long night the disciples spent fishing. You labor through the chill, even while others rest, only to find your net straining nothing but water at dawn's glow.

A long night can extend for years. You cast your net to this side, then to that; still, no answer. You know that fish can be caught in this great sea of prayer. You've heard reports of answers to prayer from others. You've even had your own. But this night is a serious, dreadful night of need. Your earnest pleading is met with heart-deflating silence. The taunting slap of waves against the side of your boat seems to say, "You're wasting your time. Why pray? There are no answers coming. No fish are here!"

Dawn comes. It's time to move on to something else, you think—like sleep. Suddenly you realize there's a man on the shore, unrecognizable in the glare of the sunrise. He cups his hands around his mouth and calls, "Throw the net over the right side and you will find some."

Your response at this point may be, "Who are you? What do you know? I already tried that side numerous times. Go away!"

Be careful how you respond. No one ever knows how or when the Lord will come with his answer. Often you won't recognize him. He may come to you as another tattered fisherman just meandering along the shore. The Lord may send his answer through a raw, unbelieving sinner. Listen carefully to the voice at dawn, even if you don't recognize the figure on the beach. Remember, all things and people are at his command.

The disciples obeyed a man they didn't know, a man who told them to do something that defied a whole night's experience. There were just no fish. Still, over the side went their net. Their eyes widened and muscles bulged to draw in 153 large fish, an overload that would normally break the net. Their simple act of obedience led to two vital things: result and relationship.

What was the result? Probably a big fish give-away. When God blesses his people it's to empower them to bless all around—much like a tree that provides clean air, shade, and fruit, not for itself, but for creatures to enjoy.

What was the relationship? Breakfast with the Master led to a deeper call to "Follow me and feed my sheep." Imagine that!

Often you may attempt prayer but don't make it to the dawn, never see the stranger on the shore, never hear his command, never have breakfast with him, and never receive his greater call. What happens then? Discouraged and fatigued, you row to shore in the middle of the night, give up, and go your own way. In short, you stop praying. Of this you can be sure, however: The Lord will not strand you at sea. There's no such thing as praying without a harvest.

Keep fishing even when the night is long and no fish are in your net. Pray on until the dawn, when the obscure figure on the sand is revealed to be the Lord himself—answer in hand. Pray on until he gives you results that enable you to bless others. Pray on!

■ COMMUNE WITH GOD ■

Father, I'm encouraged to learn from this event in the life of those seven disciples. Forgive me when I allow the darkness of the night to overshadow the light of your promise. Find me faithful until dawn.

■ MAKE THE TEXT YOUR OWN ■

Day One: What key thought do you wish to remember from this meditation?

Day Two: What answer to prayer have you recently received that benefited the lives of others?

Day Three: What prayer request do you need to resurrect and faithfully bring to the throne of grace?

Day Four: What steps can you take to stay focused and disciplined in prayer when all physical signs would tell you to give up?

Day Five: Ask the Lord where you need to throw your net in prayer in order to see him answer. It may be that you're asking amiss—such as throwing the net on the wrong side of the boat. Write a simple prayer asking for wisdom and direction.

Abandoned, Never!

I cry out to God Most High, to God, who fulfills his purpose for me.

Psalm 57:2

God has a purpose for me. What a thought! What's more, it will be fulfilled. That's something worth shouting from the housetop.

Psalm 138:8 reads, "The LORD will fulfill his purpose for me; your love, O LORD, endures forever—do not abandon the works of your hands."

Why was the psalmist requesting not to be abandoned? All people have a psychological need to be worth something. People strive hard to gain a sense of value from others. In time, however, the heart cries out for a statement of value from a higher source. Nothing can rival the galactic revelation that the sovereign God has a purpose for you, a purpose that elevates you above the universe. You are God's stellar performer over creation itself. That's breathtaking!

But the psalmist cries out for God not to abandon him for a second reason: People wanted to literally kill him! "You're worthless and we want you dead," they threatened. In Psalm 57 David rehearses his escape from Saul who hotly pursued him. In Psalm 138:7 David says, "Though I walk in the midst of trouble, you preserve my life."

David's not merely contending with people who refuse to affirm his value as a person, but people plotting to take his life. In the middle of this he's able to affirm in prayer that God's purpose for his life will be fulfilled.

What about you? Get a pen and paper, and make a list of those who love you, encourage you, and help you. Now list those who resist you, hate you, violate you, and antagonize you. Don't read on until your lists are ready. I mean it; make your two lists now.

Do you see some names on your list that you believe God should remove from your life to better fulfill his purpose? Don't believe that. If that were necessary, he would remove them. The truth is each person is a player God uses to fulfill his purpose in your life—and no one can do a thing to stop that!

Viewing each person in your life as God's instrument to fulfill his purpose for you can give you a whole new understanding. Christ told you to pray for your enemies (as well as those who love you) and those who despitefully use you.

Look at the life of Jesus himself. He was surrounded by a wide array of followers, one laying his head on his breast and another plotting his betrayal. Jesus threw himself into the hands of God to fulfill his purpose through every one of them. The result? Your salvation!

Certainly you don't feel as though you can compare the purpose of your life with the life of Jesus Christ, but while your life cannot bring salvation to the world, your life can take it to the world. That's eternally purposeful!

God does have a purpose for your life. The apostle Paul lifted this idea from the psalmist and wrote in Philippians 1:6, "Being confident of this, that he who began a good work in you will carry it on to completion until the day of Christ Jesus."

To know that God has established a trans-universal purpose for you, and that no person or thing can stop it, should not inspire a cavalier spirit. But indeed there is place to proclaim with David: "Awake my soul! . . . I will awaken the dawn. I will praise you, O Lord, among the nations; . . . For great is your love, reaching to the heavens; your faithfulness reaches to the skies" (Ps. 57:8–10).

Filled with undeniable value and unstoppable purpose, praise and pray onward!

▪ Commune with God ▪

Father, my heart is strengthened by what I've seen. Keep my eyes on you alone, that I may not be drawn into defeat by ascribing to my enemies greater power than what I give to you.

■ MAKE THE TEXT YOUR OWN ■

Day One: What key thought do you wish to remember from this meditation?

Day Two: List the names of people who love you, encourage you, and help you. Thank the Lord for the positive influence these people have in your life.

Day Three: List the names of those who resist you, hate you, violate you, or antagonize you. Thank the Lord for all he is accomplishing in your life through these individuals, as well.

Day Four: Skimming the Gospels, list individuals or groups of people who resisted or hated Christ and how their words or actions revealed their hearts.

Day Five: Viewing each person in your life as an instrument of God to fulfill his purpose for you can give you a new understanding. Think of a person who has brought pain into your life. How may God be using that person in your life to accomplish a greater purpose?

When God's Just Being God

As the heavens are higher than the earth, so are my ways higher than your ways and my thoughts than your thoughts.

Isaiah 55:9

Saint Augustine of Hippo wrote, "If you think you understand, it isn't God." Indeed God will forever hold in his being vast mystery beyond our comprehension. This doesn't suggest, however, that God can't be understood. He has revealed himself. Our problem is we're so blinded by our corrupt thinking that we can't see the doctrinal nose on our face. Endlessly God forgives when we think he should judge, has patience long after our short fuses have blown, and answers prayer when we consider it undeserved.

Here's a true story that demonstrates this. One of my dreams in life is to purchase a small farm in order to establish a care and resource center for pastors. Although I didn't have the funds, when a small farm came up for sale, I couldn't help but look at it. The owner (let's call him Boyd) was exceedingly bitter over being forced to sell as a result of a pending divorce. Knowing nothing of his faith, I said, "Boyd, as a Christian, I could never be part of robbing another man's dream. If you wish, I'll donate my services to counsel you and your wife. Further, I'll pray that God will restore your farm to you."

Boyd never did call for assistance with his failing marriage. Each day, however, as I drove past his little farm, I asked God to restore it to him. I prayed with greater fervor than if I were seeking to have it for the ministry, nearly weeping for joy at times to think of Boyd keeping his farm and his marriage.

God did it! The FOR SALE sign came down one day. A friend who knows Boyd's situation told me, "Everyone wondered how he refinanced. It must have been your prayers."

Months later, I learned Boyd not only had a shady past, but since recovering his farm, was caught stealing red-handed. Human reasoning (my own included) would assume that God should have shut him down to use his farm for higher purposes. Not so with God. His grace is much too high for that. God is showering Boyd with grace on top of grace, extending mercy to Boyd long before he seeks it, or so it appears. But our thoughts are, "He blew it, so judge him now!"

Coming to agree with the heart and mind of God demands lives immersed in prayer—all of our lives. No one's but a split second away from resorting to the natural way of thinking. In Isaiah 55:7, just two verses before the text we're studying, is written, "Let the wicked forsake his way and the evil man his thoughts. Let him turn to the LORD, and he will have mercy on him."

When God says his ways are higher than ours and his thoughts above ours, it's good to seek him and comply. It's not that God can't be understood. It's that sometimes we don't want him to think and act the way he thinks and acts.

God is just being God. We need to learn to live in his ways and pray as he thinks.

■ COMMUNE WITH GOD ■

Father, I often feel at odds with you in my prayers. The reason is simple: I want your ways and thoughts to be like mine. Draw me, as I seek you, so that I can pray for people with the same grace you wish to bestow upon them, and upon me.

■ MAKE THE TEXT YOUR OWN ■

Day One: What key thought do you wish to remember from this meditation?

Day Two: List the attributes of God that are revealed in this week's meditation.

Day Three: When you see "evil" people prosper, what goes through your mind?

Day Four: Read about Saul's (Paul's) life prior to his conversion in Acts 8:1–3. What character traits would best describe Saul?

Day Five: God's love can penetrate the hardest of hearts, just like Saul's. Reflecting upon Paul's amazing conversion, think about what God desires to do in the heart of the one you consider to be an enemy. Why not hold that person in prayer today, allowing God's forgiveness to flow through your heart?

The Final Prayer

Amen. Come, Lord Jesus.

Revelation 22:20

*I*t's said that you came into the world with nothing and so shall you leave with nothing. Not true! You came into the world with nothing, but you will leave with the record of your life. While you enter the kingdom as a free gift of God's grace, it's the record of your life and service to Christ that will establish your position in the kingdom (Luke 19:11–27).

The year that lies before you is like one chapter in the book of your life. It has 365 blank pages. You'll write the story that will follow you into eternity. Write a good one, and write in such a way that the Lord will say to you, "Well done, my good and faithful servant. Because I found you faithful in a small matter, take charge of ten cities."

Television networks run year-end recaps of global news. It doesn't take a prophet to know there will always be scenes of bloodshed, broken treaties, wars, earthquakes, fires, tornadoes, hurricanes, floods—in short, grief added to grief. The Bible says that the efforts of evil men and the travail of nature will increase as the end draws near.

This will be true until the Lord returns for the Battle of Armageddon where he will destroy the armies of the world, then enter Jerusalem, the coming world capital, to establish the kingdom of God on earth.

The darkening clouds warn that the storm is coming. But they also promise it will pass on "that day" when the Son of Man appears.

Until then, your work is clear: "The Spirit and the bride say, 'Come!' And let him who hears say, 'Come!' Whoever is thirsty, let him come; and whoever wishes, let him take the free gift of the water of life" (Rev. 22:17). Your task is to invite the entire world to come. "I tell you, now is the time of God's favor, now is the day of salvation" (2 Cor. 6:2).

Pray earnestly for the advance of the gospel, the message that invites "whosoever will" to come to God's salvation in Christ. Indeed, you have many people and things in your own life to lift before God. But underscore in your thinking the closing prayer of the Bible, "Amen. Come, Lord Jesus."

There's no other hope. You're privileged to stand in the gap and occupy until he comes. One of the most important things you can do during this time, however, is pray for his return.

Much of your work in prayer should replicate the prayer ministry of Anna (Luke 2:36–38), who, widowed after seven years of marriage, devoted her entire life to live in the temple, fasting and praying for the coming of the Christ. She could have easily said, "God said he would send the Messiah, so I'll go about my life until he comes." No, she knew that God's will in heaven gets established on earth through prayer.

Anna prayed. She was rewarded by seeing the child eight days after his birth.

God has given his word that his Son will return. In light of this, it's your calling to steadily take up the final prayer of the Bible . . .

■ COMMUNE WITH GOD ■

Amen. Come, Lord Jesus.

■ MAKE THE TEXT YOUR OWN ■

Day One: What key thought do you wish to remember from this meditation?

Day Two: How has God used this book to develop your prayer life?

Day Three: In what areas have you seen your prayer life develop over these past 52 weeks?

Day Four: With whom might you share what you've learned to assist in their prayer life?

Day Five: What specific prayer requests have you seen answered by following the insights shared?

The greatest request Ron Susek ever made to God was to pray. It's taking a lifetime, he says, but he's learning how, day by day, even though he started his ministry more than 30 years ago. Then he anticipated speaking to churches, then at citywide evangelistic efforts across the country.

Today you'll find Ron Susek not only addressing evangelistic efforts, but also hundreds of ministers, ministry leaders, and missionaries on islands from Palau, Guam, Phonpei, Majuro, and Chuuk—the Micronesian island state, where, along with training Christian leaders, Ron is writing a master plan for the governor in an effort to rebuild their civilization. (On his last visit there in Summer 2001 a police entourage escorted him to a commissioned address of Chuuk's entire government and leading religious figures on the island's future.) His speaking engagements range from evangelistic rallies and spiritual awakening conferences, to Discovering the Real You seminars and Bible conferences; a prayer team of more than 1,000 staff and volunteers uphold his ministry each day

His first book, Firestorm: Preventing and Overcoming Church Conflict, inspired a conflict mediation division. Headed by one of the most experienced mediators in the nation, the division is but one of seven arms of the Susek Evangelistic Association. The others include evangelism and spiritual renewal, Bible conferences, mass media outreach, books and videos, vision discernment, and foreign missions—all results of the Association, which formed in 1968, following a major citywide evangelistic crusade in Susek's hometown of New Kensington, Pennsylvania.

Ordained as a North American Baptist minister, Ron Susek continues to cross denominational lines. He's even received an honorary doctorate from Inalta Seminary in Jakarta, Indonesia.

To relax Susek loves to spend time with his horse, Tex, a birthday gift from his wife. But his most wonderful moments are with her, sitting on the back porch of their home on warm mornings, lazily sharing everything from small talk to deeper thoughts and dreams.

To contact Ron Susek or his ministry:

Susek Evangelistic Association
P.O. Box 3007
Gettysburg, PA 17325
Phone: 1-800-53-TRUTH
Web site: www.churchconflict.org